Nicole Moore was bo
writer, published poet,
consultant. She is the ⌐⌐⌐⌐ of Shangwe and the co-
founder of Words of Colour Productions. Nicole's poetry
writing is diverse and includes themes that explore issues
of identity, gender, race, culture, spirituality and
motherhood. Her work has been published in *Poetry Today*
anthologies and *The Weekly Gleaner* (UK).

www.shangwe.com
shangwe

Developing New & Diverse Creative Writing

ARTS COUNCIL
ENGLAND

BROWN EYES

A selection of
creative expressions by
black and mixed-race women

Edited by
Nicole Moore

Matador
9 De Montfort Mews
Leicester LE1 7FW, UK
Tel: (+44) 116 255 9311 / 9312
Email: books@troubador.co.uk
Web: www.troubador.co.uk/matador

ISBN 1 905237-14-6

Cover illustration: © Photos.com

Typeset in 11pt Gill Sans by Troubador Publishing Ltd, Leicester, UK
Printed in the UK by The Cromwell Press Ltd, Trowbridge, Wilts, UK

Matador is an imprint of Troubador Publishing Ltd

This book is dedicated to my son, Andrew.

*When will the colour of a man's skin be no more significant
than the colour of his eyes?*

Bob Marley

CONTENTS

CINNAMON: What's it like being us? Part I
POEMS

ESSAYS

INTERVIEWS

CHOCOLATE: Who do you think we are?
POEMS

ESSAYS

INTERVIEWS

CINNAMON: What's it like being us? Part 2
POEMS

BEIGE: When will our skin colour be just a colour?

ACKNOWLEDGEMENTS

My ancestors have shaped my journey and in particular my grandmother and mother who gave me a sense of a woman's value and worth. Both of these significant women lived in harsh times, through wars and a less developed British society than we live in now and both rose to their life's challenges. Both were active in improving their lives although my mother was more able to do so, and she passed down through the generations a lively and fearless spirit and a strong sense of independence. They each shared their secrets and oral 'herstories' with me, particularly my grandmother.

Mostly, I would like to thank my black sisters, who have without question throughout my life opened up their hearts and spirits and given me their undivided attention and support, and contributed towards guiding me through my journey.

I would particularly like to thank the following – Eureka Shabazz for daily dialogue through the good and sometimes rough times and who I can only say has been a wonderful friend over the years and a true sister. Thanks to Colette Machado who in those early days became my writing buddy and listened to my ideas for the anthology.

Many thanks to all the anthology contributors and to those that have attended Shangwe workshops.

Thanks to the Arts Council England East Midlands for the financial support. Thanks to Kate O'Brien, Literature Development Officer at Northamptonshire Libraries & Information Service for those supportive lunch time meetings.

Special thanks to Joy Francis, for copy editing and creative consultancy.

Last but not least, thanks to Nicki Murphy, one of the first contributors to submit an essay. Nicki has consistently given her support and over the last year has officially worked as an Arts Administrator on this project.

FOREWORD

Brown Eyes has been a revelation for me. The privilege of reading the words of such a diverse range of black and mixed-race women – passionate, intelligent, funny, assertive, modest, reflective and spiritual – has accelerated my own creative desires and personal growth.

Interviewing 18 of the 42 talented contributors brought tears to my eyes, laughter to my heart, humbled and reminded me that I'm part of a very special fraternity: womanhood.

Having the voices of black and mixed-race women within the same anthology allows you to own the differences, relish the similarities and bask in their individuality and the richness of their poems and essays. All of which highlights *Brown Eyes* as a starting, not an end, point.

So why our experiences, insights and wise interpretations aren't sought or nurtured with any value or care by the publishing industry continues to rankle. It's not as if we are creatively idle.

An estimated 72 percent of black people read for pleasure, claims a 2003 study by the Arts Council England and Office for National Statistics: 11 percent more than Asian people. We have an above average level of participation in creative writing. Within a one-year period, 7 percent of black and 10 percent of mixed-raced people had written stories or plays compared to the national average which stands at 4 percent. The list is endless, shattering every illiterate stereotype, particularly the one that says 'we don't read', in its statistical wake.

I have yet to meet a black or mixed-race woman who hasn't written, isn't writing or planning to write. I have yet to meet a black or mixed-race woman who doesn't have 'another' career (an undercover literary one), fuelled by the unfathomable, and often suppressed by fear and over-protection. From what, you may ask? From misrepresentation, from rejection, from misunderstanding, from envy – rage even – not just from the white mainstream, but from 'our own'.

Many of these women, whose courageous words are embedded within these pages, mirror this experience. Andrea Levy, already a seasoned writer when she won both the 2004 Whitbread and Orange 2005 prizes for her literary miracle *'Small Island'*, understands this all too well.

Back in 1999, she is reported as saying: "Publishers have a herd mentality. They were worried that I'd be read only by black people." And after winning the Orange prize, she clarified her position: "None of my books is just about race; they are about people and history."

That herd mentality can be both a blessing and a curse for black and mixed-race women. Publishers still point to Monica Ali (*'Brick Lane'*), Zadie Smith (*'White Teeth'*) and Helen Oyeyemi (*'The Icarus Girl'*) to signal their slow growing racial awareness. All three authors are feted. All are youthful. All are, more significantly, Oxbridge-educated.

The subliminal message is that a privileged education (combined with youth and a thick fictional slice of minority ethnic 'lifestyles') equals mainstream success and credibility. Who, then, are these books really written for? Is this elite route into publishing a way of sustaining what Toni Morrison calls the "White Gaze"?

She has said: "No African-American writer had ever done what I did – none of the writers I knew, even the ones I admired – which was to write without the White Gaze. My writing wasn't about them."

I'm not remotely suggesting that being a black or mixed-raced woman who has graduated from Oxford or Cambridge means your voice isn't 'authentic' – of course not. We know they have worked twice as hard to get there. But when these are the *only* voices plucked out, elevated with ease, and financially nurtured – mirroring the educational background of many high profile white authors as well as the composition of publishing itself – awkward questions need to be asked, and answered. I'm sure Andrea Levy, who received overdue acclaim in her 40s, would be first in line.

Some of those 'awkward' questions are now being asked by the Diversity in Publishing Network (www.diversityinpublishing.com), launched in February 2005. It is beyond coincidence that the network's concerned founders are black (Elise Dilsworth, an editor at Virago, Time Warner Books), and mixed-raced (Alison Morrison, head of marketing at Walker books).

Meanwhile literary projects like *Brown Eyes*, developed and published independently of the mainstream, will continue to have resonance and meaning. We *know* where these women writers are. We *sense* the untapped depth of their talent, originality and vision. We are no longer waiting to be selected. Instead, the groundswell for change through direct action, facilitation and networking is taking a shape and life of its own. It's exciting, it's live and it's our time.

I'm proud and honoured to be part of that renaissance, and I give soulful thanks to the likes of Verna Wilkins (founder of Tamarind Books – www.tamarindbooks.co.uk) and pioneer Margaret Busby (this country's first black woman book publisher), for laying the crucial foundations in the UK. Nicole Moore, Editor of this anthology, is continuing that legacy.

Toni Morrison encapsulates with great astuteness what it is that we, as black and mixed-race women, have to offer – and gain – as poets and writers. I'll leave you in her capable and inspirational hands.

"I really think the range of emotions and perceptions I have had access to as a black person and as a female person are greater than those of people who are neither.... So it seems to me that my world did not shrink because I was a black female writer. It just got bigger."

Joy Francis

INTRODUCTION

Being a lover of books quite late in life (it took me until 1995 to actively pursue reading black women's literature, which I identify with and enjoy), I soon became frustrated at the lack of literature written by – and for – black and mixed-race women in the UK.

My decision to create this anthology was personal and political rather than academic. The aim was to discover new and diverse talent, ensure representation and act as a medium for black and mixed-race women to speak out and reach a much wider audience.

The aim was also to promote poetry and autobiographical writing of black and mixed-race women from African and African-Caribbean backgrounds, and offer everyone the heightened perspective available to those who come with 'new' eyes.

Brown Eyes is my first anthology and my ambition is to produce another two titles, subject to funding – watch this space! This is extremely important 'work' that I am committed to continuing one way or another as I realise a particular calling. I am also only too aware of the fact that writers of colour, particularly black women, find it harder to get their work published than their white counterparts.

As well as being a contribution towards Black British literature, *Brown Eyes* is meant to celebrate, reflect upon and embrace our diverse female identities and the common-thread that unites us living the UK experience.

This rare and exciting anthology brings life to a host of talented writers who share their individual voices and perspectives relating to gender, race, culture, heritage, ethnicity and identity. I feel sure that many female readers will identify with and be inspired by what is shared within the text.

As you read through the book, you will discover just how diverse the contributors are and that they evolve from a vast array of cultural backgrounds, which influence their identity and lifestyle challenging the many singular definitions of self (especially the stereotypes) within the monotone world by extending boundaries and definitions. You will also deepen your understanding of issues affecting black and mixed-race women at large.

Working on this anthology has been a real joy. I have thoroughly enjoyed the whole journey from the early days of sounding out my ideas with close friends to the initial advertising for submissions through to receiving and selecting the contributions, which were of a high literary standard.

I have received excellent feedback too from many women who thanked me for *"flying the literary flag for women of colour, because we have a wealth of unheard talent which deserves to be exposed and enjoyed by the masses"* (Louise Hercules, 2005).

In the early days I had a good vibe about what I was trying to achieve, and it has evolved into a truly wonderful project. The breakthrough came when I received financial backing from the Arts Council England East Midlands as then I felt so much more confident and focused on the work, which I knew deserved to be supported in this way. This meant I was able to work with the support of a valuable team rather than in isolation.

I am particularly pleased that I was able to reach and include creative writing contributions from women nationally so as to represent black and mixed-race women's writing from a UK-wide perspective.

All the contributors to this anthology start with the writer's sense of self and a commitment to sharing their journeys. Join us as we embark on a much-needed exploration of our varied cultural heritages, our ancestral and spiritual connections and our personal testimonies of life in England.

Nicole Moore

EXPRESSO

Why do we write?

Poems

Independent Mother

Breadwinner
City Slicker
Father Figure

Head Teacher
Love giver
Determinator

Chief Examiner
Trendsetter
Peacemaker

Freedom Fighter
Inspirer
Empress & Impresser

There is none other like an
Independent Mother

Holly Abrahams

Unconquerable Innovators

Labelled as primitive sub-human fools,
Erased is the history of when we once ruled,
But in memory lives on our creative tools,
For centuries our heroic spirit was despised,
Our past achievements minimised,
And equal status denied.

The 4 m's, Garvey, Luther, X & Marley;
Wheatley, Parks, Truth, nanny of the maroons,
Davis, and other so-called uncivilised coons
All helped to pave the way,
Demanding the right to our say.
Revolutionary resistors of foreign ideology
They fought against prejudiced policy
Striving for freedom & democracy.
They rejected the term minority,
For their blackness they made no apology.
Teaching us not to run or hide,
They stood firm, filled with black pride.

Pioneers of science and technology,
Masters of mathematics, medicine and astronomy.
Did you know that we first invented the 365-day calendar.
Light bulbs, traffic lights and toilets?
Did you know that we were the first
To perform surgery on brains?
Did you know that we designed aircrafts,
Spacecrafts, telephones and trains?
Lewis Howard Latimer, Jane Wright, Dr Patricia Cowings,
Fredrick Mckinley, Matthew Henson,

And the rest of those they forgot to mention,
Thank you all for your invaluable inventions.

Kings, queens, prophets, musicians and artists,
Our titles form endless lists.
Africa, from Egypt to Ethiopia,
Was and is still the world's greatest utopia.
Despite demonic dictators and nigger haters,
We remain unconquerable innovators.

Tonya Joy Bolton

Black on Black

Hey Black man!
Come here; let me hold your hand.
Let me tell you about when the ocean met the sand.
A metaphoric prediction of our union,
Set in place when he; our father, said let there be ...
Do you believe in destiny?

Hey Black man!
Come here; let me talk to you.
Let me whisper soft words of yellow and baby blue.
Let me speak sweet silence in your ear
and in silent words and still motion,
experience all that it is to love me;
Black woman.

Tolu Melissa Carew

Black – History – Month

Black History Month,
Race past time,
Culture learning period,
Political events worldwide

Black History Month,
Diaspora roots calendar,
Negroid ancestors' diaries,
African-American learning February

Black History Month
Recognisable dates 31 days UK,
Outstanding archives passed on,
Strong people time

Black History Month
Colourful events lunar,
Common dates calendar,
Popular people worldwide

Black History Month
Unique revelation time,
Of colour passed down forever,
Mweusi Historia Mwezi

Christine Collymore

Origins

Yes, track me the scent of my skin on a coast off Paramaribo
where a trade wind blowing its precious cargo
doesn't know that one day they'll build rockets
from behind those trees and aim for the moon
where this Captain is sailing his ship by the stars

Trace me that line of ancestors on that shore
Ibo, Hausa, a Madeiran fisherman drawing his nets off the reef
waters that flowed from Chechnya and the Nile
one single ice-flow melting
down from the tundra

I am listening for the soft pad of a footfall morning
a Yamomani and Macusi morning
a grand-fathers-who-don't-know-their-name-yet morning
skins melting into ochre forests where young men
are rubbing tinder sticks in the sun
and women drape skins even as you

dropping soft-pawed from the rocks
spine bristling with porcupine quills
into new centuries of prayer flags and eddoes
and turbans mimicking a call

land on the prow of this ship
and watch the Captain as he stares at the stars
thumbing his salt-water map
his wolf-eyes holding the moon

Yes, track me the scent of my skin on a Paramaribo morning
where an archipelago whispering the rosary
calls so enticingly.
But, tread water, wait
I don't wish to arrive yet, not just yet.

Maggie Harris

The Quay

When swelled with the acrid scent of musket blooms

I shall assume you have defected from the shallows where you hide
As if to rise,

Gather choice pieces of yourself and smear them blind beneath my
chosen suns

Until they, eager to feed siesta skies indulge your skin as you recline
into ever redeeming rhythms that soothe you

Ensue to remove you from a black-eyed groove so tight,

Where spotlights engaged us and moments of unbridled confusion
unfolded themselves to be

To be there.

To be shrouded in the gaze of those so ready to slay your hand from
mine

Just like their summers were designed on the anklets of our
fall…from grace

A favoured place in which they'd gladly step into the riches that
we've built,

Without a trace of guilt or consequence or reason but to keep our
minds confined in altered states

Until we'd break, soften then to bow from all the sanity we vowed,

So let them gnaw and let them scavenge if they choose

For you and I will never lose

The art of keeping fiends at bay.

Louise Hercules

Redefining History

We, our parents, our grandparents, came to this country
And in half a century, redefined Britain's history

Invited to pick up the pieces of a post war Britain life was tough
They were promised employment that was plentiful if they went
And so to avoid dire poverty, they came on board ships to see
If they could make some money, then return to their beautiful countries

Arriving by ship enthusiastically, they were greeted by the mist and
the grey of the sea
The bitter cold of the winter season, was nothing compared to the
ice cold freezing
Attitude, of those in this country, full of hatred and hostility

Greeted by signs of keep Britain white, they'd come unprepared
for a fight
No dogs, no Irish, no blacks, they had to always watch their backs
They were told this was the mother country, what mother uses
terms that are derogatory
What mother rejects and sets out to inject a sense of worthlessness
within the child she should caress?

For 50 years we've struggled and fought, sometimes defiant,
sometimes distraught
To make a place and be accepted, as young (or old) and black and gifted
And look what we've achieved, despite having to live aggrieved
We've excelled within this land that refused a helping hand
Despite the fact we were deceived, we came and we achieved

We built and developed the NHS, made London Transport one
  of the best
Established a carnival while we were oppressed, that's now renowned
  as Europe's largest
Facing fascism and humiliation, tackling racism and discrimination
Just look what we've achieved, despite having to live aggrieved
We've excelled within this land that refused a helping hand

In spreading the word of the Holy Scriptures, in trade unions
  and in literature
In sports and politics, in broadcasting and music
In entertainment and education
We helped empower this nation
Despite the fact we were deceived, we came and we achieved

We, our parents, our grandparents, came to this country
And in half a century, redefined Britain's history
Redefined Britain's history

Zita Holbourne

Sharp Talking

Mi on a journey wid mi pen
carving out mi identity
trying to find out – who is me?

De English language is mi weapon
de standard dat pushes doors open

Mi caant believe it for true.
Mi caant use dis mismatch lingo stew
wid meaning for
mi feeling.
Da diction don't stretch
caant reflect
mi rich ancestry
from many countries.

Mi want mi vocab
to cut tru' de lies
wid razor sharp syntax
dat wrap up de domination
and fling it back
wid determination

Mi want de power
to control de final hour
when mi get recognition
for mi unique creation.

Sheree Mack

'African Roots'

Talking about Africa, Sea, Sun and Sand.
Oh my gosh, what a beautiful land.
Palm trees, mangoes, lots of fresh fruit.
These are some pleasures that we found in our Roots.

The Roots Festival, oh what a journey to behold,
You will experience your history, as the story unfolds.
Add a new chapter to your story of Life,
As you will remember our Ancestors' strife.

Stolen and battered, chained and flogged
Stuck in a hole, treated worse than dogs.
Flung in the Ocean, because of dead weight.
The ship was straining, no more could it take.

Treated like cargo, exported as slaves.
Oh what very good servants we made!
Children, women, our elderly too.
They didn't care what our people went through.

As long as they'd have some profit to make.
It didn't matter which family they'd break.
All were chattel to be bought and sold,
They tell us now our story is old.

"That was in the past," they like to bleat.
"It wasn't us who were the robbers and cheats!
We didn't do it, so don't blame us!
We really don't know why you're making such a fuss."

Oh really, really, then what about the Jews?
The Holocaust is never far from the news.
Hiroshima? Oops, lest we forget.
"That was just an accident of our nuclear test!"

Well history will speak for itself!
Our history we will now take off the shelf.
To pass it on, for our generations to tell,
Of how our people were condemned to hell.

Let them know how far we have come
And how much work is yet to be done
So to all of my brothers and my sisters,
Let us put straight all the mind twisters.
Let the truth stand firm and let it stand strong
As we remember how they did our Ancestors wrong.

Nelissa Mendy

My Poem to you ...

O mother of mine
I'm so proud of you
So proud to see
Your pictures in papers
Your face on my screen
Your presence on stage
To know all you've done
To watch as **you** grow
Helps me to know
Why I love you

Sweet mother of mine
You are to me more
Than a queen of
Inspiration
Dedication
And education.
What I have in you
Is a friend like no other
Not just a mother
And I thank you

Hot! Mother of mine
You hold inside you
A fire that burns
Eternal passion
Which I hope will never
Be extinguished by
Your aquarius waters.
I'm blessed as your daughter
And I'm glad.

Angela Morton

Standing on the Block

Head bowed
Eyes lowered
Limbs shackled

Joined together by the oppressor's fetters
Strength, Pride, and Hope
enduring through interminable suffering.

Remarkable
Unbreakable
Unquenchable

Myrle Roach

Images of Womanhood

ACT 1

Sitting, staring into the mirror
The vague image becomes suddenly clear.
Embryo, infant, toddler,
Mama's helper and Daddy's princess
Manifested into one
As a lifetime journey goes on.

ACT 2

Sitting, staring at the treasure in your arms
A real life breathing image.
Expecting, needing, demanding
Your precious gift to you.
Born from your own expecting
Bringing a lifetime of needing.

ACT 3

Sitting, staring, past the mirror
Blurry images go flashing by
Conception, creation, completion
A lifetime of questions pondered and unanswered
Confronts mortality with the ultimate resignation
That the journey goes on.

Myrle Roach

Antique Roadshow Revisited

a jail hidden
behind the rotting wood
of a Kentucky tobacco farm
one stop in the
transcontinental network
of holding pens, jails & yards
a warehouse of human traffic

this slave ship
turned upside down
on the banks of the Ohio River
that fickle water, smelling of freedom

Kimberly Trusty

My Heart in Africa

'Home is where the heart is,'
I guess my heart is there,
Far away in Africa, where I should be
Year after year.
I've felt the breeze, the gentle breeze, the softest ever blown.
I've seen the trees, the plants so green, the greenest ever grown.
I've felt the Sun with warming grace – the warmth puts a smile
  on every face.
I've seen life and people so beautiful. I've heard the black kites
  morning call.
I've received smiles that touch your heart, I've seen sights that
  sparkle your eyes.
The love I've felt makes you laugh, makes you cry.
The love as deep as the African night sky.
I've experienced where my true roots are, but why so far?
Over the seas and through the night, there to awaken to the
  African skies.
I swear by the stars above, I've never felt so much love,
For the beauty leaves a trace, I've found my resting place.
And I will sleep and dream of the family that I've seen.
I'll wait and hope and pray that I'll return soon someday.
The rains wished us farewell, the rivers rapidly swelled.
The wind breathes your name, says you must come back again,
The Sun touches your hand – home in your blood land.
'Home is where the heart is,' my heart and soul are there,
Far away in Africa, my blood land
I belong there.

Ony Uhiara

Brown Eyes

The Conflict

"She was calling me"
Just like a mother to a child,
"Mama Africa"
Beating African drums through my mind,
"But I ignored her"
For to her my heart was playing blind,
"'Cause I adored her"
The other mother that my life was signed, "For she taught me"
All I was, redefined my mind,
"And she brought me"
Into this woman I grew to find,
"Yet deceived me"
Mother London who I grew to love,
"Wasn't real in me"
So was this woman really who I was?
"Was I adopted?"
From the mother of children from diverse breeds,
"And united"
With children who grew from diverse seeds?

"Mama Africa"
At last I've learnt to take heed of your cry, "Mama Africa!"
I understand now where the truth lies,
"You enlightened me"
Taught me the truth of which you are,
"You corrected me"
The daughter or your maiden name Ghana,
"See you in me"
The reflection of you in me can't be wrong,
"But who are you'?"

I can't perceive the sound or your drums, "Unfamiliar"
My lips can't word the lyrics to your song, "All unclear now"
Have we left this union far too long?
"Losing focus"
Why can't I identify with your ebony face?
"Mama Africa"
Mother London is all I've known in your place, "I am different"
Raised in the life of my other mother-land, "But persistent"
To keep you now I've found in my hands,
"Black beauty"
Your love has captivated my being,
"Black essence"
Your smile has elevated my living,
"In my heart"
You'll remain, with everlasting pride,
"Mama Africa"
I love you, in spirit, truth and mind.

Lynda Wireko

Interviews

HOLLY ABRAHAMS

"I define myself in simple terms: Black British. I am Nottingham-born and bred. I've got family all over. My parents are from England and my grandparents are from Jamaica. They have been in England for years now.

I've always been encouraged to celebrate my culture within my family. My friends are the type of people who acknowledge who they are as black people and acknowledge their heritage.

I've been writing properly since the age of 11.

By properly I mean writing prose and songs. During 'A' level English I wrote an article on Black British music and how, at one point, it was connected to gun crime. One of my teachers said that I should send it to a newspaper as an opinion piece, but I didn't.

I made a breakthrough with my poem *Independent Mother*. The poem celebrates the strength of the mother; the strength that women embody in their personality and presence. It represents many women. The absence of father figures stood out for me when writing it, and how a lot of women have to fill their place when they are single parents. They can't, but they try.

I'm doing an Arts Foundation Diploma before taking a BA in Graphic Design. When I finish I want to own my own editing company and establish a magazine for young people. I want to help to get young people from the community into art and design as a career.

When I was growing up I found it hard to associate with any up and coming contemporary designers. That's why I want to do something that combines my writing and my designing.

Finding Black British writers is hard. I've read quite a few books by

Diran Adebayo. I loved 'Some Kind of Black.' Panya Banjoko is a Nottingham-born writer and poet who I also enjoy.

I struggle to find books about my age group and I'm always looking for books by Black British authors. Even people I know who are in reading circles find it hard to recommend any books.

I was doing a project recently on black beauty and how black women are portrayed in the media. They often have to change their natural beauty to fit into the stereotype of beauty within Western society.

A lot of people, even those who aren't black, think of Beyonce in this context. They talk about her hair being blond as a sign of her compromise. I disagree because black women have always experimented with their hair colour.

Although it is liberal in the UK and black people do have a strong identity and culture, I think it is hard to get into certain professions and jobs. Within the performing arts we are not considered as strong actresses compared to our American counterparts. Black actresses are much more mainstream over there. Even Black British actresses are excelling, like Marianne John Baptiste who stars in 'Without A Trace.'

The literary and artistic worlds are already established, so not compromising my writing style and Britishness will be hard."

DOROTHY CORNIBERT DU BOULAY

"I've had stand up rows in a major bookstore over their black section. They argue that they have the section so that black people know it's there. Don't they think that black people know their A-Z to find an author? Is it only black people who read black books? I love Margaret Atwood's prose and I read Toni Morrison, the supreme diva of literature.

I first put pen to paper five years ago when I co-wrote 'War Inna Babylon', a screenplay with my younger brother. I got as far as speaking to a couple of production companies, did a reading at the Institute of Contemporary Arts with some actors. But for several personal and political reasons I abandoned the project. 'War Inna Babylon' was my practise, my training as a writer.

For years I was a publicist and a promoter in the music industry. I'd always write things such as press releases, so elements of my work have appeared in newspapers and magazines.

I started teaching English about three years ago then switched to teaching English Literature. It opened up a whole new world for me.

I started writing again this year. I've got a forthcoming novel called 'Black Man's Blond', which is about skin shade, culture and identity in the post colonial society. It's one of the labels I've had to endure over the years.

Although we are free and black, we have this gradation as given to us by the coloniser which makes me a blond because I'm Creole, Carib, French and African. My mother is Jewish and African-Caribbean. My father is St Lucian, but he is also mixed. He is half Carib, a quarter African and a quarter French.

What I notice is that if you are a quarter white it is irrelevant, but if you are a quarter black it is somehow significant. That is a left over from the inventory of slavery. As far as I'm concerned my mother is black and my father is black.

The idea for '*Black Man's Blond*' came to me after reading Franz Fanon's biography. It was the first time I'd read any of his work and I was mesmerised, especially when he spoke about the dependency on the former coloniser and that black people are always looking for approval from that coloniser, even when they have been decolonised.

When I was writing my book, there was a furore over Halle Berry winning the best actress Oscar. In America she was black, but in England they were saying she was not black. When I look at her she isn't white. Most people see her as black because Halle says she is black.

My essay for this anthology, *Searching for a Black Jesus*, was influenced by these events. It is not literally about Jesus being black but is a metaphor about searching for some salvation within the whole context of being black. It was quite liberating to write.

Being a black woman living in London and having a voice is a very special gift. There are certain avenues for us to make some change. We can be pioneers. I feel like a pioneer and hope that *Searching for a Black Jesus* provokes debate."

PORTIA MSIMANG

"*Black, Actually* was easy to write because it's something I feel strongly about and had given a lot of thought to but never really had a chance to say except on a one to one basis to certain people.

The essay is about my experience as a Black Briton. It is a reactive rather than proactive title. We don't go through life thinking in terms of race and colour in relation to ourselves, we think of ourselves as other things like a writer, lawyer or mother. To me, I've mostly been forced to think in terms of a racial identity because others require it of me.

Fundamentally my mother is white (English-Welsh), my father is black (South African) and I consider myself to be black. From my earliest days I was told I was black. I had never heard of this mixed-race thing until much later. I don't think it is a very positive label for any of us.

Black, Actually is about where does black begin and end, and become something else, and how black do you have to be to identify as black? The term mixed-race is an extension of the shade hierarchy, which is very ugly. It is a colonial thing. I don't think we need it or should subscribe to it in the here and now. Ultimately, it divides black people.

In apartheid South Africa, and in South Africa today, they call people coloured and mulatto. It is a way of saying I'm not black but one up from being black. But we are all black, and if we are going to destroy this notion that there is a shade hierarchy we might as well say we are black. To me it is a dangerous game to play.

My father came here seeking political asylum. During the apartheid years it was very clear that our major struggle was against that racial hierarchy. His argument is that it is the people who chose to call themselves coloured who built apartheid. I don't want to be the person who builds it here.

There is a lot of anger and guilt related to that and now it is a big part of who I am. How that relates to what I write and how I write it – I don't think I've done enough creative writing to say.

Black, Actually is the first piece of work that I have submitted for publication that is about me rather than about something else. The fact that it was accepted was exciting for me and has inspired me to write more. By writing more means that *Black, Actually* is something of a cornerstone to build other writing around.

I don't read that much fiction. Possibly the most inspirational writer for me is Angela Davis. In terms of fiction, which resonates long after reading, it would probably be Dostoevsky. Angela Carter's *'Nights at the Circus'* is my favourite book of hers. She is the closet thing in English writing to magical realism.

There is also *'Indaba My Children: African Folktales'* by Vusamazulu Credo Mutwa. That is a good book. These are my father's people and they are very against writing down their history; it's oral history.

My dad knows his oral history going back hundreds of years. But I don't know the language so he cannot repeat it to me."

DESIREE SENIOR

"I find black writing so complicated or oversimplified sometimes. We have two ends of the spectrum with nothing in-between. At one end you have the emphasis on material gain with the bling-bling mansions and sex. At the other end it is highly spiritual, about knowing your roots as a black woman. There is no middle ground for books you can read comfortably without worrying about whether you go to church enough, are spiritually aware enough and have enough money.

I want to read books that I can identify with and relate to. I've written poetry for my family and special occasions. I added a poem to my university dissertation and received really good feedback. So I thought I should take writing more seriously.

One of my first poems to be seen publicly was written after the birth of my daughter Micah Sankofa in 1998. When it was passed around family and friends, I would be asked to write poems for special occasions like a christening or a nephew's birthday.

Hot Bread is the first piece I've sent off anywhere. It is an essay, which is a departure for me. I really enjoyed writing my dissertation and as a civil servant, I write a lot in my job. I wanted a change, though. I had a story to tell about my childhood, about being mixed-race, and my journey as a writer.

I grew up in Mitcham, Surrey. I was one of three black children at my school. At that time it was a predominantly white area. The area was known for BNP right-wing activity and there was a lot of racial tension.

In the past I would be asked 'are you half caste?' I identify myself with me first, not with a colour.

My mum is Jamaican. My dad was born in Jamaica to a Scottish dad and a half Jamaican- half Scottish mother. My dad has bright blue eyes and is very pale. My mum looks African with really high cheekbones. I have really plain features. I really wish I had full lips and prominent black features.

On forms I always put mixed-race. It is hard to say that you are black or white. There is Chinese on mum's side of the family. So I tick a range of boxes and see what they come back with.

Socially I've noticed a change in how white English men relate to black women. They find black women very attractive and seem to want to be in their company.

I've not been overly impressed with the style of writing in the books I've read. Ben Okri's 'The Famished Road' is one of the exceptions. I like to read Iyanla Vanzant, but I find her writing very heavy sometimes. It makes me feel a bit out of the loop as a black woman. But I do think that she is inspirational.

For poetry, I associate myself with the singer/songwriter Jill Scott. I was writing poetry similar to her lyrics before I heard her, which is encouraging."

LYNDA WIREKO

"I was raised in Harlesden, London. You see the ghetto and how hard it is to succeed. I left when I was 15. It was like being in a bubble. When you get out of that bubble you can reflect. When I was living in Harlesden, you went to your friend's house and stayed there until all hours of the morning. That was your life.

I'm living in Harrow now. I've made some white friends. When you are in Harlesden you just stick with black people.

I still have friends in Harlesden but my mindset has changed. I don't want to say that I look down on my friends, but I see things differently now. I'm trying to get them to see things like how I see them: that we can better ourselves; we can be stronger than the community. We don't have to rely on benefits and state welfare.

The first poem I wrote, *Product of Our Environment*, was about that experience. I was 18 when I wrote it, and it was published in an anthology called '*By the Light of the Moon.*'

In 2003 the *Voice* newspaper published my poem, *Power of a Woman*. I was so elated as I'm trying to get myself out there as a poet. I thought maybe there is a chance for me to be a writer.

You don't really know how good your work is until other people read it, people who are not your friends, but outsiders who don't have to take your feelings into consideration.

I wouldn't say that I've read a lot of poetry, but you don't really see the perspectives of black women in general publications. Our experiences and way of living are different to other cultures.

The Conflict is a poem about an identity crisis. I came to a point at 20 when I didn't feel like a British person. So I went to Ghana, where my parents are from. I loved it, but I didn't really feel Ghanaian. They didn't really see me as Ghanaian, just as a foreigner, a British person.

Although I know my roots, I can't deny the fact that I am British. I was raised for 22 years in London. My mindset is totally different from how a Ghanaian would see things.

I'm halfway through reading Martin Luther King's biography. I'm also very, very keen on reading the bible. There is so much wisdom."

CINNAMON

"What's it like being us?"

Part 1

Poems

All Dressed in...

Long dress, short dress,
Got to look good, got to impress.
Long hair, short hair,
Does anyone really care?

Keep fit, lose weight,
Exercises I just do hate.
Two or three tiers,
Plenty of tears throughout the years.

Hen night stag night.
Morning comes will both look a sight.
Will the groom arrive?
If not I will (NOT) survive.
Gold ring, white ring,

Three hymns to learn to sing.
Two or three thirty,
Don't be too late, groom get shirty.
Our way, or their way,
24-hours is a very long day.
To heel or not to heel,

I'm 4 foot 4 what's the big deal?
Uncle Bob, Auntie Flo,
Invite people I don't know?
45, 250,
Trying not to be too thrifty.

Black car, silver car,
Could have walked, not that far.
Sit down, stand up,
Real ones or plastic CUPS.
"White, cream, purple or blue,
I don't know dear, it's really up to you.
Although I think blue is amiss,
Peach would make the day oh so bliss."

1,2,3,4,
Months of stress, can't take anymore.
Really, really got to be *sure*.
The wedding is all I talk about, am I a bore?

Correct me if I'm, wrong, but isn't it really my day?
So am going to have things my way, MY WAY!
I stand corrected; it's the groom's day too.
But honey, darling, you will do what I want to do?

Bisi Akinola

Puppet on a String

Confined to a goldfish bowl
& forced to play the role
Of the good dutiful wife,
I gained a husband, but lost my life.

For years I stayed quiet
& didn't even control my diet
Forbidden to leave the house!
I became a reclusive, timid mouse.

I worked & worked while he spent & spent,
Until he gambled away all our rent.
Each night I worried & wept,
While he partied with girls he kept.

Come what may I'm leaving him today.
No longer will I serve & obey.
He's had his fun, now it's my time to play,
& voice what I have to say.

But whose gonna cook mi dinner
  & wash de clothes?
whose gonna pay de bills
  & blow de pickney dem nose?
Whose gonna keep mi warm ina bed
  & bury mi when mi dead?
Whose gonna keep de place clean
  & carry mi when mi lean?

Not I, go ask your dirty whores,

Or learn to do your own domestic chores.
Now move, & let me through those doors.
You're a grown man & a dad,
Stop acting like an irresponsible lad.
I'll send for the children once I've settled down,
then you'll be free to roam the town.

> *you won't geta penny off mi. You ugly bitch!*
> *you'll come crawling when I'm rich.*

You nu see se mi bags dem pack,
Trust me, I won't be back
Look at your face twisted with greed.
god & myself are all I need.

Farewell you lazy good for nothing jerk,
I'm off to do my kind of work,
Free from dictation
& objectification.

I've wasted years being a puppet on your string,
Now I'm gonna spread my wings & sing.

Tonya Joy Bolton

The Unseen Women Workers

We celebrate the unseen women workers,
Past, present & future
Slaves, factory workers, nurses, mothers, housewives, teachers,
Dressmakers, hairdressers, carers, cooks, cleaners & church leaders.
We honour surviving sisters with blistered hands,
Working overtime to meet family demands.

But please find time
To shower yourself with the love you deserve,
To nurture your dreams,
To weave your own destiny.
To iron out any obstacle,
& paint the world with your unique vision.

Women of every age, occupation & race,
You are called to recreate a new space.
Women of the world,
Every grandmother & girl,
Unite at this sacred hour
For we are born to liberate & empower.
Women of every shape, shade & size,
Now is your time to reclaim & rise.

Tonya Joy Bolton

Neo Soul Brother

He's as cool as the breeze
Always wanting to appease
Me…
He's relaxed and at ease
Knows for sure, about the needs
Of a woman like me
He's kind, he's sweet
Looks a little rough, but he's neat
Tall, dark and handsome
One of a kind, not really random
He's a breath of fresh air
Something that's very rare
To the type that I usually adhere
To…
He's a comfort to the eye
The heart, body and mind
Like a visual piece of art, it's divine
Like the sun and the moon, it's precise
I kid you not, this guy's so nice
Educated, and aware of the past
A humble man, who controls his wrath
A gentle man, with a soothing laugh
Smile, and a gripping touch
Knows his role, which I love
So much…
He's passionate and confident like no other
The reflection I love to see in the mirror
The one to nurse me instead of a doctor
The thought in my mind pass every hour

The essence I require inside a lover
He's real, he's the one, my neo soul brother.

Monique Campbell

One Night

It was cold outside, a winter's night
Inside was warm, his comfort, a delight
Arms amid the body, thoughts shared
Flickers of light on tanned walls, and in the air
Artistically the candles melt, our love was felt and embraced
Track six of Chico Debarge *The Game*, still plays
Lips are pressed, and fluids are exchanged
Sensual thoughts, and names are renamed
"I love you," he said, and I said it too
I said it again later, because I really do
Not like the love I've had before, but something bran new
He says he feels the same way… Phew!

The wind knocked boisterously at the window
Increased the blaze and we cuddled up closer
Track was on repeat, so kept on going
So did we…
Hours went by and I sighed
Not for anything other than the warmth in his eye
That coincides with the pleasure in mine
It was a cold winter's night
But we were radiant and alight
Phosphorescent and brilliant
We were in love and it was alive
Temperature, aura…just right.

Monique Campbell

What's Love?

What's love?
A means of segregation
An excuse for passion and emotion
A convenient exit from isolation
Or the sole reason for confusion...redemption
What is love?
A walk in the park...maybe in the dark
A butterfly evolved from a caterpillar
An offspring emerged from its mother
The consistent beauty you see in one and no other
Or the reflection you see in the mirror
Is that love, what you see?
Or is it who you hate to be?
Can you really rule out the possibility?
Is it love...is it me?

Monique Campbell

Identity

I once was a slave but now I'm a leader,
an African Queen with the world on her shoulders
my beauty outstanding, my laugh, attention demanding
I am a Queen.

I walk with rhythm, I talk with rhythm, I dance with rhythm,
...I am rhythm.
A Queen with jazz in her fingers is who I am.
Oh you play jazz? Well I am jazz.
So you like blues huh? Well I am blues.
So soul's your thing? You're speaking to her.

For my voice can caress, my voice can be strong
my voice can be tender; my voice can be passionate
I am versatile.

I am a natural actress, a natural singer,
a natural dancer, a natural athlete.
However do not be mistaken, I am all this and much, much more.
I am a natural healer, a natural teacher, but above all I am a natural
mother.
Yes I said I am a Queen.

I walk with pride and dignity.
Sophistication and sensuality.
My eyes the colour of rich soil, my skin in over 12 shades.
I am beautiful; I am a Queen.

I am unmistakable, irreplaceable, unforgettable; I am a Queen.

I am beautiful, attractive, charming; I am a Queen.

I am desired, loved, adored; I am a Queen.

I am bold, spirited, and audacious; I am a Queen.

I am wise, intelligent, brilliant; I am a Queen.

I am admired
I am envied
I am scorned but still a Queen.

I am hope.
I am soul.
I am the voice of all black women and I–am–free.

Tolu Melissa Carew

Home

When I put my arms around my lover
And I kiss his face
I am home.

When I put my arms around my lover
And I kiss his face
and he puts his arms around me
in a sweet embrace
I am home.

Not home in London but in Lagos.
I am walking through Surulere with the sun on my face
I am eating suya, listening to Fela and Sunny Ade.

When my lover kisses me
and lays his head against my breast
I am in Victoria Island, Biaduo.
I am 10.
I am running and laughing
with tears streaming down my face
my cousins are chanting, the parrots are squawking
the fathers are talking
and the mothers are yelling
E rora *(Be careful)*
E ma subu *(Don't fall down)*
To ba subu wa jé gba *(If you fall I'll beat you)*

When my lover calls out my name
I am in Sunnyfield's
I am rolling through sand

I am no respecter of time and place
I am a child, I am eight.

When I touch my lover's face
and I stare into his eyes, I am six.
I am walking through Badagri with my family by my side
I am safe, I am warm. I am four.
When my lover places his warm hands in the small of my back
I am climbing up mango trees and I feel free. Now I am three
and I have not left that place called trust.
My mother is singing "Where have all the young men gone"
And when my lover reaches that place
I am brought back to those feelings I thought I had lost.

I am 10, I am eight, I am three
I am two, I am one
I am reborn.

Tolu Melissa Carew

CINNAMON: What's it like being us? Part 1

47

The Diaspora

Send me forget me knots, I forget her not
She stands central and large
Her beaming rays transcend brighter days
Her offspring, I in far pastures raised

Her dispersed seed across the oceans
Evolved into a beautiful life,
A stranger, survivor through the motions
A champion, conqueror through the strife

Importing gifts as we come
Attribute to each and everyone
Talents, colour strength and flavour
Thank her kin for this favour

Assimilated to new ways
Yet united genetic core
Kwasa-Kwasa Congo drums
Rhythm we rock the floor

Sturdy structure, sturdy hair
Afro, twist relaxed or braided
Mustard, mahogany & malted brown
Melanin forever shaded

Express life love fish and chips
But Sunday dinners never traded
Fried plantain, sweet jollof rice
Tasty top A graded

Royal brethren overseas
Students, workers and refugees
Exiled for a season or forever gone
Mother dearest to you we belong

Amanda Epé

My Mother Came to this Country

My mother came to this country
To find the fortune in which she believes
My mother came to this country
Hoping to escape bad memories

My mother came to this country
To find her way
My mother came to this country
But not to stay

She arrived on a ship, on a cold foggy day
Ended up in west London, looked for somewhere to stay
She rented a room and searched for a job
They said they could only pay a few bob

In sixties London she was pretty wild
Then she found out that she was with child
The father was white, my mother was black
She lived with him still, despite the flack

The names she was called cut into her deep
At night, when alone, she'd break down and weep
In the day she was strong and held her head high
She loved her pale baby with big dark brown eyes
She ignored all the racists, she didn't care
She loved her pale baby with ebony hair

The strength that she had, she fed to her youth
When the father walked out, she told her the truth
That things would be hard, but they'd just have to cope
Turned out of their home, she still lived with hope

Where society failed her, she lived for her girl
And hoped that she could make a place in this world

My mother came to this country
Hoping that she could achieve
My mother came to this country
Hoping that she would succeed

My mother came to this country
And turned mentally insane
My mother came to this country
And to her dying day remained

Zita Holbourne

Fine Pass Me

Accent of the Freetown region of my mind.
Family region, before regimented England.
Mixed Freetown fathered
And mothered too, but
Northern born I am, northern born I grew.
Dialect the deed of favour
Sounding so free
Fine Pass Me.
Her generosity – over the phone.
Just in three – words.
Another woman giving her reason
To rasp in tune
With my thirsty memory
Her bloom of meaning, being
My unforgiving fever
About behaviour

Bombastic urban dowry
Trying to claim me
Mining at my mug shot
Manhood, sisterhood insistent
To covet their mistress race
I sleepwalk in the face
Of one relevance coming
One scenery – out of me.
Just in three – words
Fine Pass Me
Their hotline
To be the heartbeat
That I leave behind.

Emma Louise Felicia Hopkins

Mourning!

I lost my
beautiful comely exquisite rounded substantial derriere
In Middle Rock.
In Middle Rock where blows were hot
I couldn't stop to cherish my
beautiful comely exquisite rounded substantial derriere.

In Middle Rock I was caught between
rocks and hard places.
But nowadays we don't mention these disgraces.
No! Not nowadays.
No! Nowadays we keep schtum.
But Lawd knows I sacrificed so much,
because pain was hot in Middle Rock.
Yes! In Middle Rock pain was real hot.
Sometimes, I want to turn back the clock -
not for the sake of Middle Rock,
but to stop the passing of my
beautiful comely exquisite rounded substantial derriere.

When I see derrieres in rhythm,
Treasures of Mali, Benin and Songhai
Derrieres like rolls of laughing thunder,
like dancing shades of fierce sunshine -
derrieres awakening memories in the recesses of my mind.
I recall gathering of moons in naked splendour
like birds of paradise in natural flow.
Then my Middle Rock bile rises thick
and blisters bitter bitter bitter.
I mourn the passing of my treasure

and shed tears for the loss of my
Beautiful Comely Exquisite Rounded Sacred African Derriere.

Jackie Lewis

Essays

I AM.....

Amanda Epe

The early days

My parents settled in a reserved suburban district in north west London when they emigrated from the West African countries of Nigeria and Ghana. They purchased a house in a predominately white neighbourhood. There were a few Asians who had migrated from East Africa, and even fewer families of African-Caribbean migrants who were my parents' close friends. They were our first black experiences in England.

It was here that I was born, the second of four children. I remember my parents saying there was so many of us – three girls and a younger brother.

We were quite well known on our street, in our school and at our church. A family like ours must have represented something unique at that time, in that place. But why so? We lived and behaved like every other family in the area, with our daily routines, apart from inside the house where the cuisine incorporated international foods from the more tropical regions as well as English dishes. The sounds that rang around the house echoed the bilingual literacy of my parents.

The 70s scene

Childhood in the seventies: carefree days, yet not totally so. I remember spending time alone, deep in thought; hoping to change things, change myself! My parents say I was a happy, almost too friendly child.

Starting primary school was a highlight for me. I settled in well and made many friends. In fact I was a novelty child. As I was 'different' most girls wanted me in their group, to sit at their table or be their best friend. But it was only when my friends said, "I want you to come to my birthday party, but my mum said no blacks allowed," that I became aware of racial identity.

My social and emotional development was affected by the relationship between my genetic make-up and the environment in which I lived. God didn't answer my childhood prayers during my quest to be someone else. It was later on in life, when I met other adolescent African-Caribbean females who shared my childhood experiences of identity, that light was shed on the subject.

They had grown up in schools where they were not in the minority, but they too wished they had long flowing locks. They saw the blond-haired, blue-eyed dolls that were advertised on TV; they read the books at school with images of Caucasian children. We had no images to identify with so we imagined ourselves in that media portrayal.

I was still special, though. The chart-storming African-Caribbean pop group Boney M had a hit with 'Brown Girl in the Ring'. I was centre of attention and was placed in the ring for everyone to sing to in the playground. No one fitted the bill but me.

I had taken the occasional verbal abuse from my peers, however — on many occasions — I was still the novelty child, the one who went home for lunch and on my return was swarmed by the 'fan club'. By the time we were in junior school many children had changed and had learned that my race could be used against me.

In a dispute, they would call me derogatory names about being black. Maybe it was the warrior in me, passed down by my ancestors or was purely self-defence. Whatever it was, I got into a lot of fights, reinforcing the stereotypical view in the teachers' minds of 'the aggressive black child'.

My parents backed me up. They justified my actions of self-defence when my all white peers were ganging up against me. Enough was enough. I laid my cards on the table and desired to be among those I could relate to and feel valued by, without the need to defend my existence.

In the fourth year of junior school, now known as year six, secondary school representatives arrived to show us a video of their school. On screen I watched other children with physical characteristics resembling mine. My older sister was already at this school: my heart warmed.

I remember the joy and my pulsating heart as I watched the video footage. I hoped to go to that school. My problems would be solved, I thought. I fantasised about my new heavenly environment, although I already was in heaven but didn't know it. Most of the time, it was a phenomenal experience being in a minority. Pupils who were my friends always celebrated my racial difference and wanted to be in my shoes.

The infinite ladder of adolescence

During my teens I awakened to new cultural encounters. My African heritage played a large part in my development during my teens. On the one hand I was a happy-go-lucky, everyday 80s London girl. On the other, I was under the impression that we, the family, were heading East, back to Africa. We were not British after all – we were Africans! Without the language and with limited culture and ideologies, me, my sisters and brother were fully fledged Africans returning home.

Maybe my parents perceived that British children didn't show adults the respect that they were used to. They also experienced difficulties in finding housing and employment. So this country could never be home.

"If you dare lay a hand on me social services will be on your case," I threatened. Poor dad was trying to sustain order and discipline while

I crossed cultures at home. I knew in the Western world liberty and power lay in the child's hand. His threats were idle in Britain, although dad never hit me in my life.

School was the European culture; home was the African heritage. Thankfully mum had memory failure when it came to training her girls in culinary skills to please our future husbands. Instead she taught us cooking as a survival skill.

My African-Caribbean friends, most of whom I met at secondary school, initially schooled me in Black British culture. I found them strong, determined and grounded in their cultural identity. Many African parents took their children back home to their origins during secondary school. We were among the few left behind.

At secondary school I met so many interesting black girls like me, but it wasn't all plain sailing. I never actually arrived at the heaven that I was searching for among the girls that I could, and still do, identify with. Being African had its knock-on defects.

The rumours, history, politics and images portrayed then – as now – promoted ridicule of that identity. At primary school I was placed in a circle for my white peers to sing to and celebrate. At secondary school the circle I stood in was for my own black peers to jeer at me, and it hurt.

It was difficult for them to accept my heritage, although I felt that they knew that we were all one race divided by decades and the Atlantic Ocean. In my late adolescence it was difficult even for me to accept my own heritage: wanting to go to all night parties. The curfew was on until I was a university graduate.

Post-teens I was forever climbing the ladder of adolescence.

The Equation

Almost a decade after leaving school I arrived at the motherland. Home sweet home – my first experience arriving at Port Harcourt city, Nigeria. The dense green land and red soil; a terrain blessed with an abundance of natural resources.

The change of sky – bright blue with a piercing sun, colourful birds flying across it, echoes of them singing, so much noise and people everywhere. Then came the tropical rain showers, but it was still scorching and moist. All these beautiful sights and feelings, and I hadn't seen my family yet.

Emotions were high in the family, but I was never able to openly express mine. But the day I met my extended family I wept; we wept, and wept and wept. Tears of joy fell as we united and embraced our long lost and newfound family.

Letters, phone calls and oral stories were the links that had, so far, kept us together. There was a lot to learn for someone who was African by name, but not by action. I was ready to embrace it all, lived every minute of the day and utilised those sticky eternal nights catching up with the lost years. I now felt complete as a person. The emptiness had gone and I had experienced – and recognised – both parts of my culture.

Ironically I had been called 'white' in Africa, like so many others who leave or visit from Britain, Europe and America. "Oyibo" was a nickname for us all. I fitted in very well, knew the diet, the greetings and courtesies, but we were still the famous "Oyibo". So am I as white as they think? Am I the African that I was brought up to be or the British-behaving girl? The African-Caribbean? The Black British? I am… I am… I am…

I am, and have, a complex, novel and diversely created culture. I have missed opportunities to sit on grandma's lap while growing up. I have missed the the extended family support and celebrations, something that is highly valued in my African culture.

I have definitely missed the sun and bountiful tropical fruits, and have poignantly lost on growing up in my roots because there is no place like home.

I have missed much and gained a great deal. In London I appreciate many cultures and have become intercultural. I have had the advantage of freedom and freeness, education, healthcare and celebrating the equality of gender. Most importantly, although my parents detest this act and would not allow it, I am a first generation that escaped the dreadful ritual of female mutilation. That, for me, is complete jubilation.

HIS PRECIOUS GIFT

Tina Tamsho-Thomas

Even as a small child she was fascinated by mirrors — and everything else that reflected light.

Her mother's proudest stories of her babyhood tell how she stood up in her pram at her grandmother's house and made up calypso songs about the mirror on the chimney breast, the fire casting shadows around the room, the cut glass trinkets in the display cabinet and the shiny brass ornaments that adorned the mantelpiece.

When she was 15, staring into mirrors fascinated her. Not because she was vain, in fact she believed the left side of her face was ugly.

She was walking past a large department store in town one day and caught sight of her left profile in the plate glass window. She must have seen that side of her face before, but it wasn't the half of herself she recognised: the features were too strong, the cheekbone too high, the protruding lips too…lippy!

She never met her father, but she knew he was black. He came to England in the 1940s to study medicine, economics, law — or something. He came from Nigeria, Africa, but he was never described as African. African was too strong, too high cheekboned, too protrudingly… lippy.

She didn't know who taught her that. Her mother's Irish family? Her teachers? Television? The books she read?

She had Catholic tastes in literature: 'Peter and Jane,' 'Mary Mouse,' 'The Bobbsey Twins,' 'The Borrowers,' 'Heidi,' 'Little Women' and 'Black Beauty'. Innocent enough, surely?

Although she never sat round the fire in 'Uncle Tom's Cabin', she knew African hair was described as 'nigger wool' and the heads of slaves were bowed in constant servility, their lips drawn wide and red in hideous caricatures.

His Precious Gift.

When she was five, a Roman Catholic American priest told her mother she was a sinful woman, and that her daughter had to accept the racist taunts of classmates.

When her mother questioned the priest's judgement, he said: "Ya shoulda thought of that before having 'relations' with a nigger."

Her mother replied: "Jesus said, suffer the little children to come unto me."

The priest held open his study door and, in his Deep South accent, blasted: "The sins of the father..."

When she was 15 she tasted alcohol for the first time. Afterwards she felt strange and unreal. She climbed the stairs and stared at her face in the bedroom mirror. Staring into mirrors fascinated her. Not because she was vain – she was afraid she no longer existed.

The blurred image at first confirmed this. The room was in darkness, but the landing light shone behind her. Her face, blurred and shadowed, fascinated her. The image in the mirror fascinated her. She turned her head to the left and studied first her right then her left profile. High cheekbones. She lifted her head and stared at her outline: beautiful high cheekbones. She studied her profile in light and shadow, shadow and light. She studied each side of her face at an angle. Beautiful, proud, high cheekbones.

She hadn't meant to look for her father in the reflection. She hadn't meant to look for anything, but in the light and shadow of her bedroom mirror, she found the proud, black, beautiful part of herself.

Her precious gift from Africa.

Her precious gift from him.

Interviews

JACKIE LEWIS

"I see myself more as a storyteller. I used to work in corporate management until 1994, and then the opportunity presented itself for me to take redundancy, which I did. Afterwards I took a Diploma in Counselling.

At the end of the course, all the students had to give a presentation, so I searched for a way of telling my story and chose to do so through poetry.

In 2000 I had two poems published (*Five Slices a Day Please* and *When Dora Fell*), as part of a project I was working on with Southwark Black Women's organisation.

Since 1995 I have tended to share my poetry through recital rather than publishing. It wasn't until I submitted poems to this anthology that I thought about why I hadn't gone through the process of sorting out my poems for publication before.

Wondering Rose is a poem about homelessness yet it is also about more than that. When we talk about homelessness we see it as someone not having a roof over their head. But I experience homelessness as not having a clear identity, not honouring myself and not feeling a sense of belonging within my family or neighbourhood.

When it comes to the black female identity in literature it's not only Black British women who are missing from women's writing generally. We are led to believe that African-American women's voices are heard. But when I think of the size of the black population in America, and the authors that I can immediately call to mind, I don't think it's that wide really.

What is really important to me is that I'm not the 'other', but that 'I am'. The 'other' is that sense of having to fit in with somebody else determining what I fit into.

This doesn't arise within me in the same way when I travel to the Caribbean and Africa. My parents are from Barbados, and I was born in Barbados so I like the sense of being at home. There's a sense of freedom that allows me to be who I am in these countries.

The feeling of being the 'other' in the UK manifests itself in that I have a part time private psychotherapy practice, and I also work for an agency two-and-a-half days a week. When I think of my work setting, the 'other' manifests itself in that I'm the only black woman in that setting.

If I was the only black woman and I had the power to hire and fire, I'd feel a sense of power, of being able to assert who I am. But I'm not. There is someone else who is in charge of that setting. For me it is about reclaiming myself not as a Bajan, but as an African woman.

When I think of the inspiration for my poetry, I go back to my childhood influences such as the musical giants the Mighty Sparrow and the elders who were never direct in chastising you. They would always have some parable to hand."

ONY UHIARA

"I started to write poetry after getting into trouble at school. I was sent out of the class, but instead of standing outside the room like you are supposed to, I wandered off to the school library, which is weird for me because I hated going in there.

While rummaging around I found 'A Midsummer Nights Dream'. I loved it and it inspired me to write, especially poetry.

I've got the IC3 anthology edited by Courttia Newland and Kadija Sesay. I love the poetry. I'm really into Toni Morrison at the moment. But I'd like to see more accessible books written by black women that everyone can read. I've not been really drawn to women's literature, but I have a thing for very old books. I go to charity shops to search for the oldest books like ones printed back in the 1900s. My shelves are full of them: 'Tess of the Durbervilles,' 'Wuthering Heights,' 'The Collected Works of Lewis Carroll'. I've always loved Shakespeare and the Bronte Sisters.

I also like fantasy stuff – I've got the Lord of the Rings Trilogy. As you can tell from my anthology contribution Secret Fairies I'm quite into fairies.

The only thing I've had published was when I was 11 while I was at boarding school in England for a year. I wrote a poem and it went into a book, I was told, but I never saw it. It felt really cool, but I have no proof.

I live with my parents, who are Nigerian. I usually go to Nigeria every three to four years. When I go I take loads of scrapbooks and notebooks and I come back with so much material.

What I find hard are the Nigerian ways of doing things including the fact that are you are supposed to get married.

A little while ago, my parents had some visitors over from Nigeria. I cooked dinner without thinking it was anything special. Halfway through the meal, one of the guests asked if his son, Charles, could talk to me.

I was washing up in the kitchen at the time, so I said, cool. When Charles came in he was sweating. I thought he was ill. He chatted away and at the end of the conversation he asked for my number. When they were leaving, Charles's dad asked me if I took his son's number. I said, no.

What happened was the last time I was in Nigeria, Charles's dad had seen me and thought I would be good for his son. So they had flown all the way from Nigeria to check me out. My parents didn't tell me so I was totally unaware. That sort of thing annoys me.

I do feel pressured. I'm like 'let me live my life please!' But whenever I go to Nigeria, I love being there especially when we spend time in the village where my parents grew up. It grounds you. It's such a different world.

It's just the duties that I'm supposed to know how to do as a Nigerian woman that are difficult."

CHOCOLATE

Who do you think we are?

Poems

QuaintUniqueElegantExtraordinaryNatural

I am strong I am bold
I come from a special mould
I am sexy I am sassy
And always, always, sassy.

I was born to be loved not to be abused
Treat me any differently then I will feel used
I am patient; I am calm, very rarely loud
I will always hold my head high. I will always stand proud.

I wasn't born to serve, cook and clean for you
If you don't like my attitude, you know what you can do
I refuse to be treated like a slave
I will hold that feeling until my grave.

My eyes are in my head not in the middle of my chest
I thought you were different, different from the rest
You get treated how you want to be treated, that is what I was told
Well, this woman is going to be treated, nothing less than gold.

I will only ever walk beside you, not two feet behind
Don't think that because I'm a woman, I haven't got a mind
Don't think of trying to change me that would be a big mistake
I am what I am, doing what I am not, is fake.

Regardless of whether you are brown, black or white
Being Queen is not a privilege, but a God given right
If you show me your love and care
You know I'll always, always be there.

I am Q U double E N
I tell myself this again and again
This belief can never be taken away
This Queen 'B' is definitely here to stay.

Bisi Akinola

History X

Descendant of the rebel tribe
Struggled, free from chains to survive
Proud Maroon, roots unknown
X marks the spot
Where thousands lost their lives
In a desperate attempt for Freedom

Today I remember my Ancestors
And realise I have a long way to go...

Jewish blood runs proudly through my veins
Oppressed race inflicted with pain
Stand naked in the showers awaiting the acid rain
Never again...

Generations passed, races begin to
mix and merge,
breaking down doors, collapsing boxes
Ripping off labels in a furious
attempt for, change
In reality the reason is simple

   Love

Here I stand today, Proud
Proud of my History
But desperate to have my own Story to tell

Daniella Blechler

Wondering Why?

The times we spent together,
The fun and happiness.
All I see is sadness now
And I wonder why?

The love we once shared,
Was it just a disguise?
All I see is sadness now
And I wonder why?

We used to hold each other tight,
To ease pain and sorrow.
All I see is sadness now
And I wonder why?

We have two lovely children
In whose future, we must take part.
All I see is sadness now
And I wonder why?

You deceived and cheated,
And I believed all your lies.
All I see is sadness now
And I wonder why?

You wanted us to separate,
To break up the family.
All I see is sadness now
And I wonder why?

As a black woman with children,
We shall continue to be strong.
There's no need to see just sadness now,
And I no longer wonder why.

Christine Collymore

Afro Britons

African, African, black, black
Yet sporadically I raise the Union Jack
Diligent citizen am I
Birthright justify, why deny

Dual identity infusion
Split by two but no confusion
Novel culture have I
Birthright justify, why deny

Urbanite or bumpkin
We doin' our ting
UK culture has started to bling
Novel cultures have we
Birthright justify let us be

Constructors, Britons built by ancestors' sweat of hands
Obligatory to own some UK land
Diligent citizens are we
Birthright justify let us be

African, African, black, black
Nought contribution to the Union Jack

Amanda Epé

Lips

My lips seem to amuse Esther.
She forces this shrill, tinny sound through hers
which then bursts into a big, rough snort. Sounds like a horse.
She says my lips are chalky and dry. Big and rubber.
She laps up laughs from the others like a drunkard needing a drink.
Maybe my lips are big, as she says. It doesn't make it any easier for me
to open them up and answer her back, though.

She always chews gum.
I always know when she's going to say something nasty to me.
Her lips mash up and down, hard,
parting and closing like a bored camel. And she's looking at me.
Laughing to herself all the while. By now
the rest of the class are flicking fingers, swaying and beating table tops
to the rhythm of her horse sounds.
She's firing out the words between each crack and slap
of the old, soured gum in her gob:
"dry, rubber lips".

I was in Jamaica last summer. Granny swears by Vaseline.
She doesn't need any of them fancy-fancy creams or lotions.
Just Vaseline. She looks so young
and always has a ready-made smile on her lips.
If my lips were ever dried or slightly cracked,
She wouldn't tell me. She'd just say
"come darling!", scoop up a bit of white jelly -
smooth it over my lips with a protective touch.
The heavy sun would just melt the Vaseline
and keep them plump and moist. All day.

Then as I'd run off, Granny would tell me
to take time and talk good with my lips.

Perhaps that's why I can't say anything to Esther now.

Patricia Foster

Undefinable

When you look at me, what do you see?
An individual filled with pride and dignity?
When you look at me, what do you see?
An individual facing up to my responsibility?

When you look at me, what are you seeing?
Do you see a person, simply a human being?
Or do you see me as a woman, or somebody's wife?
What assumptions are you making on how I live my life?

Do you see me as being on the darker side of white
Or do you think I can't be black, because I'm much too light?
Do you see me as half caste, mulatto or mixed-race
Or am I simply an individual who holds herself with grace?

Do you wonder at my age
Why I'm not wed or at least engaged?
Do you cast a critical eye or do you wonder why
I have a child and no wedding band?
Do you think you can judge me, by looking at my hand?

Do you make an assumption on where I dwell
And wonder if I'm doing well?
Or expect me to sign on every two weeks
Just because of the way I look and speak

Does my career make me middle classed
Or am I working class because of my rearing and past?
Am I classless because I am unique
Or does being like no one else make me some kind of freak?

Do you see me as a statistic?
Is your assessment of me realistic?
Why do you prejudge me, from the way I look?
Don't judge me by my cover, open up the book

Do you have the right to ascertain my colour, culture or creed
Is it not for me to decide and for you to follow my lead?
Don't look at me and decide who you think I am inside
It takes more to define what I comprise of
By simply opening your eyes up

I am *undefinable*, yet I am still desirable
You cannot categorise me and say
Because of a label I should act a certain way

I am classy and classless, I create my own status
For ever changing like a season
My life is not for you to reason

Zita Holbourne

In Black and White

Born of a two-fold nation
I caused quite a sensation
A mother black, a father white
I really was quite a sight
In sixties London, it was rare
People passing stopped to stare

White girl, paki, Indian, Greek
Half caste, half pint and half breed
Why does your skin look so light?
How could your mum go with a white?
Why do you look like a parki?
Why did your dad go with a darky?

Half white, half black, half caste!
How long would this all last?
I am a person, whole, complete!
A head, two arms, two legs and feet!

Born of a two-fold nation
It fills me with elation
A father white, a mother black
I'm me, I'm here and that's a fact
In nineties London it's not rare
And people do not stop and stare

African Caribbean and Caucasian
Called mixed-race, we are a nation
A mother black, a father white
At last society's seen the light

Zita Holbourne

All Mixed Up?

All Mixed Up is what I wanted to find out
Confused mixed-raced people was my doubt
Listen as I say this I'm not gonna shout
I'm hear to educate you on what being mixed is about

As a mixed-race person I'm never fully accepted
As I'm not just one colour I'm sometimes rejected
Sometimes neglected
Sometimes affected
How come I was the one who God selected?

He gave me this look of originality
With light skin, and hair that's curly
I looked different from the rest so they asked me
Where was I from, what's my nationality?
They put me into this different category
Like I wasn't like them and they wasn't like me
In their eyes there were no similarities
Mixed-race, half caste or half breed
Not fully one colour so they criticised me
Said I think I'm too nice and all this negativity
What term would you use to describe me?
As you never took the time to get to know me properly
Put aside my looks and get to know my personality
Let me get rid of this illusion in society
A confused individual, that's not me!
This is not a tale, this is reality

So before I go let me get this off my chest
I must tell you, must confess
That we like standing out and being different from the rest

With our own nationality nothing more, nothing less
So our answer to your question is of course, yes
We are proud of what we are if you haven't guessed
So it looks like we were the one who God blessed
Now confident in ourselves mixed-race is the best!

Danielle Imbert

Wondering Rose

She's a strange creature
Wondering Rose.
Her with the Medusa hair.
This feature of changing climates
Regal Black on a fractured
Landscape.
She is a wondering rose,
Yet noses frown and feet hurry fast
As Wondering Rose walks slowly past.

Rose in a wondering haze.
Is her bag filled with memories
Of treasured days?
No one cares to ask
As Wondering Rose wonders past.
Rose to elements exposed.
Has she been held I wonder – when last?

Rose with her crushed velvet skin.
Rose of the vacant stare
Rose of no fixed abode
Rose of nowhere
Rose cut adrift to wonder
Look! Yonder!
There she goes
Wondering Rose.

Jackie Lewis

A Writer's Guide to the North

They call it home,
The bitter North East.
The peat stained North East.
I've even called it home – once or twice.
On return The Tyne Bridge looms into view,
a wave of emotion invades.

Home – where is my home?

The wealth here's from a subterranean gem,
that black mass found in deep shafts.
An intense heat, cramped and dark,
reams were brought out and shipped down river.

Black clouds arid man-made mountains
marked the landscape.

Coal – the ebony King
We're alike.

With cuffed knees and nappy hair,
fists clenched, I tried to catch them as a child.
"Darkie."

I'm called now by
my neighbours, my community,
my home.

Sheree Mack

Ethnic Origin

WHO AM I?

a question that's got me thinking
I can't lie

I've only got one box to tick
but which one is the best fit

BLACK
☐

yes – used in the political sense to represent
the people of a darker hue
who can run and sing and jiggaboo.

AFRICAN
☐

yes – my great grand daddie came from ghana
travelled with brothers and sea
took a look at newcastle town, stuck around
and married a ginger Lassie

CARIBBEAN
☐

yes – my daddie was from trinidad
stowed away to the mother country
that spread the myth
it was land flowing with milk and honey

OTHER

☐

yes – that's how I'm viewed in society
in this fair city
it's a pity
they don't see the other side of me
not my right side
or my left side
but my humanity

so which box to tick
with so much of a mix

let's not conform
and be restricted by a form

Let's use and abuse the dotted line

.....................Black British of Afro-Caribbean descent.............

But the more descriptors put in place
Only entangles me further in the question of race

I'm British that's what I want to say
But that's equated with white, always.

Sheree Mack

My Life

Here I am standing here
As mysterious as the moon
And as bright as the sun
Shining out my colour

Here I am – not really black
So you tell me
Oh and not really white either
So I have noticed

So what is going on
In this busy world of
Everybody else's song
Telling me I'm wrong?

If only it was that simple
Shades of colour in any order
But white light is in the race
Diluting everyone's face
And it isn't even a colour.

So as a child with a dark face
Born as 'mixed-race'
Into the human-race
I refuse to fade into
This place I find myself

It's been a great journey
At times I screamed stop
You are missing the point
I am more than just a colour

It's my essence – my ancestral
Spirit that's full of life
Oh and what's most important
It's my life.

Nicole Moore

Other

You glimpse it again
the sheet of paper
paper full of groups
groups of ethnic origin
origin...where is mine?
black...
all the subgroups, boxes everywhere
white...
all the subgroups, boxes everywhere
a vast array of groups, boxes
hmmm...that's where I'll tick
only place I can
OTHER
Why do I have to tick other and then explain my parentage?
People still making it seem like a unique small group who are
  often discounted
Hmmm...maybe they should consider that over **40,000 OTHERS**
  exist
and every time we fill out application forms many of us are wondering
when the time will come for a mixed-race identity to be officially
recognised in a group of our Own.

Hyacinth Myers

Sistahood

Chocolate Sista
or maybe not
another brown woman
within the melting pot
who may be light in complexion
but dark affiliated yet in mind
her parentage mixed
but we are all part of mankind

For me I am black
as I am not white
my identity drawn
from society's delight
to concentrate on colour
and ignore personality
but London born and raised
which is my reality

So judge me not on where my parents originate
or the colour of their skin
I am my Self for all to see
so explore the person within.

Hyacinth Myers

Suggestions

White British mother
Jamaican father
the two key elements in my creation
born in London
as a child aware of mixed identity
it didn't affect me though until...
...Until others intrigued would ask
whether I considered myself black or white
but why did I have to choose?
suggest I had the best of both worlds until I...
explained the double discrimination theory
suggest that nice hair and light skin would bring happiness
when I was searching for inner peace within my Self
suggest society would prefer me more
when all I wanted was to be accepted
suggest it would be easier throughout my life
when I knew it would be harder
suggest I could not be conscious enough
when I knew what I felt
suggest that we as a race
MIXED-RACE
were...
less important
less than pure
less than acceptable
less 'black'
less than an under-class
less conscious to the..
      unfair
      unjust

>   unscrupulous
>   unspoken
>   imperfections that exist in any society today,
Well...I suggest people accept and embrace each other as we are all
working towards peace, freedom and equality and with over 40,000
of us in the UK
we are here
going nowhere
and here to stay.

Hyacinth Myers

Scrubbing The Black

Colonial words filter through each vein.
Like heroin remnants remain.

Memories reverberate like ripples on a pond
entwined with words of a cappella slave songs.

Still colonisers past and present
Stand tall in the glory
Living, Breathing, Echoing *their* powerful stories

The chains of emancipation weaken
As the voices of self-hate ooze through generations touching the
spirits of
Our mothers
Our fathers
Our children
Our people

Words that you can never forget

"You look like an African"
"She's got good hair"

"You're too black"
"He's got white in him"

These words you never forget

"Your lips are too thick"
"Rubber lips"
"He's a Coolie"
"Your bum's too big"

"Your hair's too pickie"
Voices echo ugliness
whilst words cut deep into the psyche

"Your neck is too black"
"Scrub it! It looks like dirt. Yams can grow"

"Stop swinging that towel on your head. Tek it off"

"Your elbows too black"
 "Scrub them"

"I did. They hurt."
"I said scrub them again!"

Scars though invisible
Etch themselves like tribal marks
on the mind, body, spirit and even the soul

"Your bottom too black"
 "It must be dirt"

 "Potatoes can grow. Scrub it"

"I have. It's sore."
"SCRUB……….IT………..AGAIN!!"

"Your nose-holes too wide
So don't forget to put the clothes-peg on them"

Etched

Words that you can never ever forget

Eureka Shabazz

Positively Thinking

So you think I'm a 'mixture' and my being is a plight,
but aren't we all a bit mixed up, so there you are – you're right.

My mother's European, English, Irish, French blood too,
her father was an army man, a soldier through and through.

First he fought in Africa, robbed her minerals and her gold,
ensured the Empire's dominance through Colonialism's hold.

Then he 'served' in India for **his** country and **his** king,
looted her rich culture, man he didn't leave a thing.

With India divided, her warm blood upon his hands,
he then oppressed the Irish in support of 'Black and Tans'.

Next he fought the Germans, thirty nine to forty five,
to rid the world of fascists? mmmm – to keep **his** race alive.

He hated every 'foreigner' who came into his sight,
kicked the A-rab and the nigger just to prove that might was white!

My Irish Catholic granny was born on English soil,
the church instilled the fear of God, to keep **its** women loyal.

At eight she was a worker in the local corner shop,
with little education, they worked her till she dropped.

When grandad came to court her she succumbed to all the lies,
marriage to an army sergeant meant strict regimental ties.

With 'Maggie' my dear grandma 13 children born in all,
but he wasn't just a racist as my mother does recall.

'Mad Sam', as he was nicknamed, was also sexist through and through,
when home from kicking foreigners, kicked **his** Maggie black and blue!

Of all their growing offspring, most of them survived,
kept his prejudicial bigotry kicking and alive.

They were narrow-minded bastards, who shared the values of the church,
pious at the altar, in the foremost pews they'd perch.

The youngest of the family, a shy girl – meek and mild,
grew into the woman, who would mother this black child.

The church condemned her as a whore, for loving a black man,
the family screamed their rage profane, imposed a racist ban.

So my father never met me, who knows who's to blame,
denied his baby daughter, on me he had no claim,

So I'm certainly a mixture, from Europe's melting pot of hate,
a product of a system, that produced this racist state.

But one thing is for certain, I am not a mixed up soul,
conceived in love, both parents,

made me absolutely

Whole!

Tina Tamsho-Thomas

A Penny for your Troubles

A penny for your thoughts? How 'bout a preacher instead,
'Coz I confess right about now I'm wishing I was dead.
Black skin,
White skin
Hit me with the truth; is it really necessary to greet me with your
boot?

A penny for your thoughts? Thanks, I'll try not to spend it too fast-
While I'm home can't go to work 'coz my arm is broke in a cast.
White skin.
Black skin
Taking our jobs. You best take your calcium if you think you can take
on this mob!

A penny for your thoughts? Does that buy me a gun or a knife?
I'll succumb to desperate measures to survive my desperate street
life.
Black skin.
White skin –
Let's teach that black bitch. We'll rape her-jus' the three of us mind –
Then sling 'er in the ditch.

A penny for your troubles? What really, what's da catch?
Not one, love; standard compensation on account o' you being black.
White skin.
Black skin
Don't take this shit. Thanks but no. I'll pay my own way, mate;
You racist git.

Ony Uhiara

Essays

INVISIBLE WOMAN

Tonya Joy Bolton

On Tuesday 9th February I left university with my friend Helen. We'd had an intense lecture that morning and planned to catch the bus back home to Birmingham.

"I don't know how we're expected to write 3000 words by Thursday," Helen complained while reapplying her scarlet lipstick. "I didn't grasp a word of that lecture," she sighed. "Oh well, as long as I scrape a pass I don't care," she added with her usual couldn't-care-less attitude.

"How do you cope with it all, Ebony, running your own flat, work and university? You always manage to get straight As. What's your secret?"

"I cope because I have to and it's bloody hard," I yawned. "I don't know how long I can do this for, though. I'm falling asleep at work and in lectures. Did you see Tony Blair on the news last night spouting on about how he supports students? The joker makes me sick."

"Yeah, I guess I'm lucky I don't have to work," said Helen. "My parents pay my rent and Daddy's buying me a car next month. It'll make travelling easier."

"It's all right for some, I guess," I teased.

As we laughed and chatted about how hard life was, how pathetic men were and about always being broke, a teenage boy – no more than 18 – boarded the bus. He carried a large bottle of beer. He opened all of the windows, lit a cigarette, and sat down a few rows in front of us.

Irritated, I couldn't decide which was worse – the icy chill that engulfed the bus or the stale stench of his sweat, alcohol and cigarette smoke blowing in my face. He guzzled down the last of his beer and threw the empty bottle to the other side of the bus. Like all the other passengers, I said nothing, hoping that if I ignored him, he and his foul smell would soon disappear.

As the bus sped down Hagley Road, I felt numb from the cold. Nevertheless, I continued to chat to my friend, and for a few minutes I forgot that the teenager was there. Then out of the corner of my eye I saw him spit, over and over again, not discreetly but aggressively, wanting to be noticed while aiming his spittle at the other side of the bus.

Helen and I looked on in disgust as the yellow slime rose high in the air like a flying slug, and landed on a nearby wall, sliding down like ectoplasm. I felt physically sick and clasped my hand over my mouth to keep from heaving. I looked at Helen. She looked at me. Both of us were appalled by his crude behaviour. Unable to contain ourselves, we burst out laughing.

It was then that he swung his puny, pale, chicken-like head around and addressed me. "You got something to say, you fucking ugly black cunt? You're nothing man. I'll fucking slice you up."

Each word slapped me in the face: one by one, burning like acid. I immediately stopped laughing. The chitter-chatter of the other passengers stopped dead. Everyone waited for my reaction. I froze.

He glared at me – hatred shooting from his eyes, but I stared back, daring him to attempt anything. I was Medusa, killing him with one look. How dare he disrespect me? I wanted to knock him out with one almighty blow, to yell, 'come on then, you racist tosser!' I searched for the words to describe my anger, but found none.

It was my friend who spoke first. I had forgotten she was there. "Shut up, you sad racist," Helen said.

He turned around and, again, addressed only me. "Didn't I warn you? Nigger! Bitch! Freak!" He paid no attention to my pretty white friend.

Brown Eyes

"No, it wasn't her. It was me," Helen shouted back. "So what are you going to do about it?" He stayed silent and carried on spitting his phlegm at the walls, like a possessed demon.

Although I was grateful and appreciative of Helen's support, I was painfully reminded of the differences that stood between us as women, the unequal positions of power we occupied in the external world. I am black. She is white. He had said nothing to her yet everything to me. He had acknowledged her as a person yet me as of an inferior colour. And because of that colour he viewed me not as a woman, but a mere female anatomy. Nothing more.

I looked around the bus and saw only white faces. They averted their stares and said nothing. Frustration began to overtake me. I prayed to God for strength. I no longer felt the cold as my hands trembled in anger, waiting for permission to defend me. I jammed my jaws shut, clenching my teeth tightly together as my warrior spirit tried to escape and assert itself.

I didn't want to become a monster or be condemned by others to the same category as this ignorant fool. I felt powerless. Hiding my humiliation, I laughed and chatted once again. Racing around my head was the knowledge that he had offended both my race and gender. Had I been white, he could not have referred to me as 'nigger'. Had I been a man, he could not have called me 'bitch'.

By the time the bus pulled into Broad Street, I reassured Helen that I'd be perfectly safe as she got off near her luxury apartment. I sat back in my seat, pleased with myself for keeping silent – the power and victory remained mine. I was proud of myself, and thanked God for my growth and development.

When the bus finally reached the city centre, I jumped up eager to get home. Suddenly, I was knocked to the floor. Struggling to regain my balance, I spun around. My eyes scanned the bus for help, but we were alone on the top deck. I screamed, hoping that someone would hear my cries, but the bus kept on going.

"If I were you, I wouldn't keep making that racket'," he snarled, waving his knife in front of my face. "Looks like it's just me and you. No one 'ere to fight your battles now."

I struggled to my feet and tried to run towards the stairs. He was in front of me, blocking my way. "Me dad always says you animals have forgotten your place and need to be taught a lesson."

"You need to get real. This is the 21st century," I said, suddenly conscious that I felt more pity than fear for this pathetic psycho.

"I don't friggin' care what century we're in. You coloureds don't belong here," he ranted.

"Oh please. I have just as much right to be here as you. At least I can string a sentence together," I snapped. "And who are you calling coloured? After all it's not me who's got a face like a beetroot!" I sniggered, remembering the poem my mother taught me when I was a child:

When I was born, I was black,
And when I'm embarrassed, cold, or dead,
I am still black,
But when you are born you are pink,
When embarrassed, you turn red,
When cold, you go blue, and green when dead.

"Yet you have the nerve to call me coloured!" I declared.

"I'm gonna wipe that fucking smile off your face!" he threatened, moving towards me.

Realising that my life was in danger, I backed away and yelled at the top of my voice. Almost immediately the bus stopped and a policeman came marching up the stairs. I couldn't believe it. The policeman ordered the youth to drop the weapon and turn around. The boy obeyed and the policeman stepped towards me.

"You alright love?"

I nodded, catching my breath.

"Right, so what's going on 'ere then?" the policeman demanded

"He attacked me," I spluttered. "I was just about to get off..."

"She's lying," the youth interrupted. "I was just getting off and she tried to trip me up. Stuck her foot right out."

"What?" I laughed. "That's absolute crap. If you believe that you'll believe anything. He was calling me names and making racist remarks."

The policeman patted me on the shoulder, as if I was his pet dog. "Now calm down love. Obviously, there's been a misunderstanding. I'm sure we can sort this out." He was so patronising. I stood there in disbelief. He was ignoring me, as though I were a silly little girl with a chip on my shoulder.

"So what started this?" he asked, still addressing the youth. He folded his arms across his protruding beer belly and rocked back on his heels. He was far more interested in looking important than doing his job. I didn't exist.

"Hello!" I shouted. He turned to face me. I looked him in the eye. "I've just told you, this youth has assaulted me racially and physically."

"Please Miss. I told you to calm down," he ordered, trying to stare me out. His condescending tone was more than I could bear.

"Calm down? I've told you twice that this guy's just attacked me and you call it a misunderstanding?"

The policeman sighed. "Let's just sit down and try to sort..."

"No", I interrupted. "I'm going to have this man done for assault. This matter is far from over, but this conversation is. I've got your badge number. You'll be hearing from my solicitor. You obviously don't know how to do your job, but perhaps the law will."

I looked the red-faced boy up and down infuriated by his smugness. He said nothing in his defence and showed no remorse as the policeman led him off the bus into a police car. I thanked the driver for radioing for help and stepped off the bus.

The city centre streets were crowded with people on their way to bars and clubs. As I turned into Hurst Street, a group of white men walked past.

"Eh lads! There's that Naomi Campbell innit? Ain't she s'posed to be wild in bed?" one of them shouted. "Fancy a shag, love? Never had a black tart before!"

The others burst into hysterics and staggered on. Ignoring them, I quickened my steps, anxious to complete my journey. I was cold, exhausted and fed up. When I finally reached my front door, a yardie, dripping with gold from head to toe, called to me from over the road. "Yow, sexy gal! Mi waan talk to yuh." He flashed his gold teeth. Before he could say another word I ran into my flat, like a fugitive under attack.

"I am surrounded by lunatics," I yelled at the walls as I slammed the door behind me.

I lay down on the hallway floor and gazed at the ceiling. The words of the drunken racist clung to me and echoed in my ears. But it was no longer his voice I heard. It was the cruel, malicious voices of my infant schoolmates, chanting together in chorus that they didn't want a nigger in their class.

I was only eight-years-old, one of only three black children in my public school. I'd realised that I was different as soon as I arrived. The other children laughed and pointed at me, touching me like a rare animal in a zoo. They'd crowd around me, pulling my long black plaits, fingering them with dirty hands.

"Can you actually wash your hair?" they questioned.

I remembered one particular geography lesson. We were being taught about where different people came from. I was the only black person in the class, so they used me as an example. The teacher poked me in the chest with the sharp tip of her ruler and called me to the front. She asked the class to point out the features on me that were different to theirs and asked them if they recognised the part of the world I came from. I stood there, feeling like circus entertainment as the hands of my classmates shot up one by one.

"Yes Michael," said the teacher, pointing to a skinny boy.

"Well Miss," Michael started, "she's got a flat nose and big thick lips. Her hair is coarse like wire, so I think she's from Africa."

"Very good Michael, well done! Her skin is also coloured, signifying the area she comes from in the world." My teacher pointed her long ruler first to a map of Africa and then at me. "She is a Negroid. Thank you Ebony. You may sit down now." She ignored the sniggers of the other children.

During school, I'd wander through the playground, always alone. The other children would often taunt me.

"Ape-face! What's it like to be a Negroid?"

"Were you in the Handsworth riots?"

"My mum thinks you should go back to where you come from."

I would run into my mother's car, ashamed of who and what I was. At home, I stared at my face in the mirror and cried, feeling cursed by my difference. I had internalised white supremacist values that crucified my self-image.

At Sunday school, I got down on my knees and prayed to God to be like them, to fit in, to be included and accepted. I often stood under the shower, wishing that the water would wash away all of my imperfections. I hated my 'rubber lips' and my 'Brillo pad' hair. I desperately wanted silky-straight hair that shook in the wind like the other girls. I loathed my 'thunder thighs' and longed to have thin legs, like them.

My mother refused to let me feel sorry for myself. She told me that I was lucky and privileged to be in my position. "Just keep your head held high and achieve," she encouraged, as I sobbed.

For years I hated her for not caring or fighting for me, and for sending me to a hellish school that ruined my life. But as I grew older, I realised she'd been fighting for me all the time, and made many sacrifices to give me the best education.

My mother said racism must be fought with education, for knowledge is power. She had two jobs, working seven days a week, until the blood poured from her hands. She did it to give me the life, the power, the access and the opportunities that she and thousands of other black people never had. Eventually, I wanted to learn more about myself, who I was and where I was from, for I was invisible in the curriculum taught to me at school.

I picked myself off the floor, went into my living room and picked up some books on black history and literature from the shelf, remembering how they'd helped me. Through these books I re-educated myself and became aware that masses of black children had experienced the same rejections as me.

To my surprise, I discovered that there had been black kings and queens; that one of the greatest musicians, Beethoven, was a black man. I learned that it was black people who invented traffic lights, toilets, and even built the mystical pyramids of Egypt. I cried when I read how my ancestors were branded and butchered as slaves, sold like cattle, and robbed of their freedom, their children and their lives. I thanked them over and over again for their sacrifices as I reached a new understanding and love for my people – and myself.

The phone rang, jolting me back to the present. It was late, so I ignored the call and got into bed. Unable to sleep, I lay there and listened to the howling wind. Still haunted by past insults, I told myself off for being so sensitive, but deep down I still searched for inner peace.

All my life I had changed my appearance to suit other people's perceptions of 'beautiful' and by doing so, I was ascribing to Western notions of beauty instead of my own. "How long will you allow others to dictate and define your womanhood?" I asked myself aloud as I climbed out of bed.

I found a pair of scissors and began cutting out my expensive European hair extensions. I didn't stop until I had removed every strand from my head. Feeling liberated, I slept well.

In the morning, in the cold light of day, I felt naked and nervous without the hairstyle that I'd kept since leaving school. Deep down, though, I knew there was no going back.

I combed some sweet-smelling African Pride oil through my hair, defining and shaping the mass of natural curls. Instead of applying lip liner around the inside of my lips so that they appeared thinner, I smoothed my mouth with lip-gloss, making it shine.

I decided I would not hide my legs by wearing one of my many long skirts, and chose a pair of orange trousers that hung in the wardrobe. I'd never felt brave enough to wear them before, because I was so conscious of my body, but I was surprised at how well they complimented my shapely thighs. I smiled at myself in the mirror, liking the attractive woman beaming back at me.

"You go girl," I openly joked, grabbing my coat.

Stepping out into a new day, I made myself a promise, speaking it aloud like a prayer:

"I am the Invisible Woman. My needs and opinions are not heard or counted. Yet I celebrate my unique difference and vision in a world that continues to silence, devalue and erase my history and myself. I see me."

MEN

Monique Campbell

Men! A strange species, no?

Though woman is derived from man – that's only if you believe in the idea of the creation of Adam and Eve – we're nothing like them. Maybe I'm just speaking for myself, so instead I'll say, *I'm nothing like them.*

I know you're wondering why I'm even bringing this subject to the surface. As always (I'm being honest here), a man's either done me wrong, bemused my intellect or hurt my ass – severely! But that's not the case here. Those are things only you can do to yourself by allowing it to happen.

No doubt we are in control of what we feel and how we feel it; what we think and how we think it; what we do and how we do it. First, we must figure out the why, and that just takes a little introspection, personal intuition even.

I'll pass on a little wisdom that someone shared with me: "It's not what you say (or do) that makes me feel this way. It's what I do with what you say (or do) that makes me feel this way." Think about it. It makes sense, doesn't it?

So, if I'm not making reference to some emotional freefall that a man's contributed to, then why this heart-rupturing, soul-stimulating, mind-compelling subject, you ask? Simple really. I just feel like making an external observation of a breed (men) that's contrary to my biological organism that is loved and so dearly needed – that's all.

OK, first observation. I was sitting on a train, Connex South Central, heading into London. I was minding my own business, reading 'White Teeth' by Zadie Smith. Fully indulged in the book's contents, even chuckling at Zadie's comical detailing of Alsana beating the shit out of her husband Samad in their back garden, I noticed (and it was just a partial glance) that the couple in front of me were pretending to communicate. I assumed they were a couple as the white female had an engagement ring on her finger, and it was the early hours of the morning — just after 8:00am.

Anyway, what was I saying? Yes, the pretend conversation. There I was, reading a funny book, only half engrossed now. The lady before me (slender form, dressed in a summery way, with long blonde silky hair, average European features and amazingly vibrant green eyes) was speaking to her other half about work commitments, and how she felt her skills were being abused in her role as a PR officer.

The man: white, middle-aged with a slight beer belly, cropped fair hair and dressed in a pinstripe navy-blue suit. He had the *Guardian* opened on the sports pages, and though his eyes were glued to its subject matter, he grunted and made noises of affirmation, which she accepted as answers to her questions.

As I said, they were having a pretend conversation. He was pretending to listen to her and she was (I would say stupid enough, but I'd rather not place a label on her) pretending that he was listening to her. To top it all off, she also pretended that his grunted responses were actually advice.

My mind started to ponder whether the communication would be the same if the circumstances were reversed. I just couldn't see it happening. For sure, this was a conscious form of behaviour. I've heard male associates discuss their contrived methods of falsely pleasing their woman. They spoke, once again of that method: appearing to be listening and agreeing with what their woman is saying, even when they're not. Are we women that bad? Or is this the strangeness of the male species?

OK, second observation. I was lounging in the park on another summer's day with a notepad and pen in hand, documenting some poetry and passing thoughts. Once again, through a fleeting glance over my surroundings, appreciating its existence, my eyes clapped on a reasonably young black couple (a real good-looking one at 'dat') reclining, like me, but wrapped in each other's arms.

Ah, how sweet, I thought, pushing the bridge of my glasses up and dipping my eyes back to the half-filled page in my possession. When I peeked up again, the female (voluptuously slender, wearing a red halter-neck – that exposed her well defined back – with a black skirt) had her back to me. They were still in an embrace, and the male had his eyes locked on mine.

Oh! I sounded high-pitched and a little embarrassed. He licked his lips and pouted them in a sensuous and highly sexual manner. *What the hell is he doing?* I thought, shocked and bewildered. I immediately dropped my head down to the page before me. The male: milk chocolate deluxe, a honed beauty in all that black entails, clothed in nothing more than denim jeans that encased each leg; a torso of definition and pulsating biceps; almond eyes with the depth of the ocean…*damn* he was fine!

Feeling the pressure of his eyes, I looked up. His eyes searched mine; still his tongue wet his lips, still they blew kisses and still his beautiful woman lay between his arms. *What is wrong with these men?* The female sensed something and caught my shaking head and disappointed face peering their way. She looked at her man's smiling face, and then turned back towards me with venom seeping from the corners of her eyes. I smiled at her to suggest that I was no threat, but in seconds she was marching my way…

"Take your beady eyes off my man? You can see that he's with me yet you're still watching him. I can't stand women like you, wanting what they can't have!" she screeched.

"I don't want what I can't have. I was only admiring the beauty of you both. Any issues you have take it up with your partner as he is also doing the admiring. Except his is adulterous," I said.

She turned her head to witness his lips – pouting, wet – and advanced his way…

Men.

TIMING

Monique Campbell

Timing!

There's something so beauteous and gracious about correct timing. It's to do with the cosmos, fate, everything. However, communication in all its forms, works intimately with language, particularly that of the body. Such definitive expressions come from the body's own parlance, yet many fail to comprehend the stance for its most basic signals. I'm gonna throw a few examples your way just so you can get a gist of what I'm alluding to.

It was late one Saturday night and outside my earlier plans, but I managed to rush and get ready to stand before the doors of the nightclub in Leicester Square, after a friend had invited me. I was enticed by the complimentary entry.

I was later than I'd said I'd be. Finding parking in the West End after 11.30pm is like trying to find a man if you're looking (I'm not, mind you) – scarce. In the end I had to go into that expensive car park, the one I liked to avoid. Once I was outside the venue, never having been there before, doubt roamed my mind: the crowd just wasn't appealing. *What the hell?* I thought. *It's a freebie. Nothing to lose, really.*

"You, over there! You're paying £15," some olive skin, Mediterranean schmuck with long dark hair said to me, obviously unaware that I was complimentary.

"Excuse me, I'm complimentary?" I explained, identifying her flaw.

"Complimentary guest-list's closed. Now will you please move on or stand out of the way?" dictated the ill-mannered PR girl.

Didn't I mention that I had the company of a female friend? Well, at this point I turned to her and she made out that it was my call. My instincts said, *hell no!* But my pride, and the inconvenience that the night had already caused, shouted back, *what the hell, we're here now.*

Throughout the night I noticed an infamous routine in how the men approached women, including me, and strangely, this was without discrimination along the lines of age or race (by the men, that is). This was it: lure – well, not exactly lure but physically draw a girl while she's in transit, ask her name and, just as quickly, her number and then move on.

Though disgusted by it all, the routine was working with many drunken white girls and one or two black women, who had stopped, kissed and done a few other things that I scorned.

One guy, an African-American, seemed to constantly loom over me, trying, trying and trying again. He wore the concept dry. At one point he said: "I just wanna know ya name. Wha's ya name babe? Wha's ya name?"

Throughout all of this, I'm bubbling and my back is to him, so I wondered what further communication he needed from my body to understand that I wasn't interested. Bored, tired and just feeling like I'd help a brotha out, I explained to him what my body language was visibly signalling, as well as the fundamentals of timing, while reading the body, that is.

Later on in the night, pondering hard on whether we should leave, my friend, already in two minds, and me still wanting to make the most out of my parking and entry fee, decided to stay. The same dude approaches again. *Again?*

"What does a brotha like me need to do to see ya ag'in?" he asked me from behind, his American accent purposely trying to overpower his distinctly African accent.

I turned to face him for the first time. I gestured for his head to come a little closer in my direction, and whispered into his ear: "Compatibility and chemistry."

Stunned, bewildered and trying fiercely to fathom the content of what I'd said, he stroked his jaw-line back and forth, and said, "But I cain't buy that!"

"Exactly!" was my response and my cue to leave.

So there you have it. One example of a man's inability to grasp the body's voice or the importance of time. Nevertheless, there are many more examples, like being in the passenger seat of a date's right-hand-wheel car. At your destination, being placed in the unnerving situation of how to exit. His body shifts in your direction while you're huddled against the trapped door.

Or there's the record deal you're ribcage-hungry for and will do anything to get. But the doors aren't opening, ears aren't hearing and everything in the universe is suggesting that maybe you're not quite ready for it. Maybe it's just not your time!

But in the same breath, when it is your time, when everything in the cosmos *is* working in your favour, when the wave has picked you up and all you have to do is ride, ride it some more and ride it hard until it collides with the water. Then, and only then, will you sail.

Allow natural forces to lead you to your destiny. It will when the time is right.

SEARCHING FOR A BLACK JESUS
The politics of skin shade, culture and identity: 1970–1978

Dorothy Cornibert du Boulay

I'm comfortable in my own skin. It feels good to say that because throughout my 39 years as a subject of the British Empire, I have been identified and labelled (in no specific order) as a half-breed, Creole, mulatto, red-skinned, brown-skinned, black man's blonde.

This labelling has been subject to change in accordance with what is fashionable. But as the decade known as the sixties became the seventies, I was just another poorly dressed brown-skinned kid with questionable ancestry. I had no idea about who or what I was, or where I belonged when I arrived with my family to live in brand new social housing in New Cross, south east London, fresh from the small island enclave of slum-like dwellings located in the less salubrious streets of W9.

I arrived without my mother, had few, if any, personal possessions and a limited world view; almost entirely reflective of that espoused by my father. As he was an equal opportunist in his approach to racism, I was consequently suspicious of *anyone who wasn't a St. Lucian.*

Apparently we weren't as important as the whites, but we were definitely more important than the rest of the blacks, *especially* those with uncompromisingly dark complexions. According to my father, *if you need two spotlights just to see their face* they were *too black.* Quite a paradox then, for a child to subsequently discover that within their wider community, *everyone* who wasn't English was simply referred to as a 'wog'.

I was six-years-old in 1971, and at the bottom of the Catholic education system, when I discovered that my physical composition – part master and part oppressed – only served to *confirm* my status as one of the dispossessed.

Around this period, the utter futility of my father's rationale — that being a Creole rendered you closer to the apex of power, somehow offering protection against the harsher aspects of societal inequalities and injustices — became manifestly apparent. If anything, my 'internationalism' often merely confused and delayed the inevitable outcomes.

They told me I was too clever for my own good, and I was often accused of being 'uppity' with ideas above my station. That was probably true. I reacted by appointing myself General of a brand new army of one. Ironically, the doctrine at its core was extracted from the religious teachings at my Catholic primary school and, more specifically, based on the premise that we were 'all equal in the eyes of God'.

In retrospect, I can now see that this somewhat precocious anger was undoubtedly exacerbated by the excessive amount of time I spent in front of the television. It became my oracle and from a very young age. I recall resenting the way it degraded me and ridiculed me: if we, the blacks, always got killed first, what chance did we have of winning this war?

But I persisted in watching and listening. At times it was torturous, but I knew leaders were out there, somewhere. Occasionally, I would marvel at footage featuring men with black berets, black leather gloves and the darkest of attitudes. I found their defiant presence on the screen liberating and empowering, sexy even.

But it was a case of too little, too seldom, because all too often we were displayed as broke pimps, prostitutes or police informants. Admittedly, as these characters were often American, it lent them certain glamour, but ultimately watching them left us feeling dissatisfied, merely confirming our status as the black buffoons and underachievers that deep down we really believed we were.

Despite these negatives and plain old invisibility, I was aware that there was *some* brilliance and greatness that looked like me because I had witnessed it the very first time I saw Cassius Clay in black and white.

His early victories generated a certain degree of euphoria and previously unparalleled joy in my neighbourhood. It spread like the pestilence amongst black people *everywhere*. While Cassius's early victories confirmed that we were, indeed, more than good at fighting, it felt like there was something else in the water, maybe the blood that Enoch Powell spoke of...

Later, when the Greatest changed his name to Mohammed Ali, he suddenly became less revered in our house. Although I wasn't informed of the specifics, that's when I knew that it *wasn't just about boxing*. But politics just wasn't being discussed. Perhaps it really was exclusive; the reserve of posh whites and a few flamboyantly dressed brown-skinned revolutionaries scattered here and there. I deduced that it was something foreign, alien for people from abroad, with access to resources; not a subject to be discussed by us: the downbeat, the voiceless, the Caribbean.

Even though I knew what lay at its core, this lack of discussion and communication left me feeling powerless. I'd seen Black Power in several formats on the television, but there was seemingly no place for it in our neighbourhood. And besides, it appeared so American, so colourful and so exotic. I just couldn't see how it would work in New Cross. I became obsessed with finding a way out and, as I had witnessed the Greatest and other luminaries such as Dr Martin Luther King finding deliverance in religion, my quest for greatness led me back into the belly of mine...

I knew that this was a potentially futile exercise. I was aware that the very *uncivilised* practise of slavery and colonisation led to us becoming Roman Catholic, and therefore civilised. But this didn't stop me from experiencing automatic recoil almost every time I came face to face with the religion's blatantly racist iconography.

Standing at the altar in preparation for my first holy communion, attired in virginal white lace so that Jesus could *wash me whiter than white*, I remember concluding that Glory probably didn't come in black.

At that tender age, I thought it a little too impertinent to question the religious representatives of God on the aesthetics that informed the blonde-haired, blue-eyed statuary, but I made a mental note to go and seek in order to find.

Several years later, I still remained dissatisfied, angered even, after continuously hearing that *it didn't really matter what Jesus looked like* and that I should focus on the *good things that he did*.

I abandoned all hope of being accepted into the Church of Rome's Kingdom of Heaven around 1976, when I enlisted in The Movement of Jah People. This coincided with me privately adopting a new Jesus who appeared to me in the form of Bob Marley. Bob suddenly became omnipotent, so much so, that in many households where Jesus was *the silent listener to every conversation*, you could be certain that He was also listening to Bob.

I remember being particularly intrigued by my father's interest in this sometimes-revolutionary music because *he hated Jamaicans*. What led to this blatant application of double standards? I wondered if it was because he communicated the fight that my father and other West Indians no longer had the strength to voice. I suspected that the 400 years of oppression had created a certain irreversible apathy, but felt a glimmer of hope because finally, people all around were starting to 'get up' and 'stand up'.

Almost overnight, there seemed to be a proliferation of other Rasta disciples, dreaded and non-dreaded, who provided additional revolutionary perspectives. My elder brother's collection of Max Romeo informed me about the 'War Inna Babylon', and Burning Spear provided me with the history that was omitted from the school curriculum. Admittedly, I had difficulty deciphering the patois in the beginning, but in no time at all, 'Jamaican' became the only language to be spoken in New Cross.

My quest for the truth also led me to the local community centre, which was known as The Settlement. I spent many illicit hours eavesdropping on the mystical rhetoric known as 'reasoning', and many further hours later with my peers attempting to dissect the utterances and vibrations of the local Rasta men.

Admittedly, at the time, a lot of their philosophy was confusing. Most of it went right over my head and I wasn't quite sure if I could ever truly belong to them due to my 'high yellow' colouring and loose hair that my relatives held in such high esteem. It was ironic really, because even the white Rasta's viewed me with suspicion. It seemed that somehow, their allegiance to Rastafari placed them outside of the whites, and although it didn't make them black, it made them acceptable.

The first outcome after many hours of listening to 'reasoning' was the confirmation that my first oracle, the instrument of Babylon propaganda known as the television, was loaded with untruths and distortion. I learned that Africa was the motherland, but how was that possible? Wasn't it a continent filled with flashy dictators who ruled with contempt for the poor and landless, and occasionally ate people who disagreed with them? If Africa was on the news, I was hearing only bad news, supported wholeheartedly by my father who told me that any misfortune suffered was payback because they were the ones who sold us to the white man in the first place...

In an attempt to clarify matters, at the same community centre, I simultaneously sought out the company of the eccentric African man who was always smartly attired, and in possession of a briefcase, but didn't really seem to have an occupation, as such. His differently accented oratory held a similar degree of mysticism, but I eventually concluded that because he was in agreement with the Rasta's, something significant was bound to happen – soon.

Myself, and many others besides, regularly began to pitch vast quantities of selected ghetto folklore against more official, accepted channels of information. My peers and I started to hold our own 'reasoning' sessions. We were becoming organised, although we weren't quite sure what form, if any, we would finally take.

Yet I still had doubts that any claims to greatness could be attributed to black people, and continued to doubt this until the Rasta's told me that *Jesus was black*. Sensing my disbelief, they promptly dispatched me to refer to my King James and, more specifically, Daniel 7: 7:9 and Revelations 1:15.

From that moment forth, I experienced what psychoanalysts would call a 'breakthrough'. I became excitable, full of questions: where would I find the church of the black Jesus? Did I have to be Rasta to join? Would I be able to grow dreads? I was reassured when they told me it wasn't just about wearing a dread because even if someone cut it off you could still be Rasta. It was something that came from the inside, from your heart.

That's when *the penny finally dropped*. Rasta suddenly became a metaphor for black. I realised that black was global. It could be panoramic, and why not? All of a sudden it came in every shade of brown and had room for all of Africa's children, including me, one of the hitherto dispossessed. And furthermore, Bob was the first person to tell me about this and his skin looked *just like mine*.

By the time 1978 arrived, I was still only 12-years-old, but had already survived a significant journey, one where I had encountered many great changes. The most profound discovery throughout this all, however, was the realisation that decolonisation of the mind was where liberation truly began.

It felt good to be free at last.

BLACK BRITAIN

Sheree Mack

Question: *How does she find her place in a world where she has no meaning?*

Answer: *Be.*

I've chosen the title Black Britain. Not because that's a place I feel I belong to. Not because I believe it is an accurate term. Basically I've used it because it's shorthand. It's quick and easy. Isn't that the way?

We people of mixed heritage use quick 'get out' clauses instead of going into our complicated heritages and histories. We make the decision for the audience or the listener, and assume they wouldn't be interested or wouldn't know where each country was so why mention details. But we still shout complaints that society doesn't listen, that society isn't interested.

Britain today is only going to learn about us – our cultures and histories – from us, when we start to tell each other.

When I'm filling in forms, for jobs or surveys, there's always the equal opportunity, ethnic group monitoring section. There's usually a Black British box to tick, or Black Caribbean or Black African. I always tick 'Other' because I don't identify with any of the above. I'm not trying to be awkward, but the question asks how I define myself. I'm a 'mixness'. There is no box to tick for that. It's taken a long journey, time and effort to come to this definition and I'm finding my way within it.

My dad was a Trinidadian stowaway in the 1950s. He came to Britain with the myth of the mother country flowing with milk and honey firmly in his mind. He was disappointed, along with thousands of other British citizens who came from the Caribbean to claim their birthright.

He was an engineer by trade, but could only get an unskilled factory job in Bradford. He worked there until he was too ill to work any more. He died when I was nine. My dad found his true love in Britain, my mum. My mum was a Geordie lass, born of mixed-race parents whose fathers were from Barbados and the Gold Coast. As I said I'm a 'mixness'.

I was born in Bradford. For the first 10 years of my life other children abused me at school because of my weight. It wasn't until I moved to Newcastle, after my dad's death, that my skin colour came into the verbal and physical abuse. Luckily, my size came to good use at this stage of my life. A kid only called me a name once. He was too scared to utter it again.

This wasn't an ideal situation to grow up in. The abuse and silence told me that I didn't belong, that I was different. However, the abuse didn't give me any indication of where I did belong in this society.

"Go back to where you come from!"

What? Bradford? Ah, they didn't mean there, did they?

I began to hate my colour. I grew up in a predominantly white society. Everywhere – from the schoolyard to the housing estate to TV to the cinema screen – there were white faces. I wanted to be white, to just to fit in. Reading books became my escape. Through imagining myself in the heroine's place, with blond hair and blue eyes, I felt at home. In that made up world, I was popular – and wanted.

When the opportunity came to move out of the area and go to university, I took it. I went to London looking for answers, to find my culture, my history, and me. I found much more than I had bargained for. I found Bettie Smith and Billie Holiday. I found Una Marston and Claudia Jones. I found Joan Riley and Jackie Kay. These remarkable women had been denied from me when I was growing up. I didn't know they existed. Learning about these Afro-Americans, Nigerians, and Jamaicans made me feel that it was more than okay to be black. It was an honour.

I came back to the North East of England to be with my family. I came with the full knowledge of my ancestors, in my heart, body and soul. I taught in a local secondary school and was the only black teacher there. I remember that words like 'darkie' and 'paki' tripped off students' tongues so naturally, like they were part of their everyday speech.

There is still a large amount of ignorance in British society. It's probably worst in areas that are predominately white. I should know. It scares me. On the positive side, I feel that I'm in a position where I can make a difference, trying to bridge some gaps in knowledge and historical connections.

I do that the only way I can – by being me.

LABELS

Nicki Murphy

'Nouns – names were the most powerful words. They strike home like a pin through a butterfly…and you're caught wriggling, staked through the heart by an identity, and no matter how much you squirm and protest, 'No it isn't like that', the noun holds you down till you set fast in the pose it nails you to.'

Maureen Duffy, 1983

Labels. They are difficult things. Classification, pigeonholing, categorising, names, types, stereotypes – all different forms of labels.

Traditionally we label something to make it easier to understand, for our own comprehension. Once we know what to call something or someone, we can file it into the appropriate mental box, retrieving the word for future use as and when necessary.

The trouble with this methodology begins when the label is interchangeable: when it is subject to frequent alteration, when it is replaced with a modernised, more politically correct version from time to time. When this occurs one must change the thought process (memory) to fit the new updated label. Perception is everything.

Half-caste. Mixed-race. Dual-heritage. For the purposes of this piece I am choosing to stick with 'mixed-race' for the following reasons: the first term is no longer PC (and also too closely related to the class or caste system of social and economic organisation in India for my liking), and the third term is too restrictive. Dual-heritage, 'dual' denoting 'two', is misleading. If one investigates even the very surface of a mixed-race person's family origins, there are usually many more than simply two of any ethnicity or nationality to be charted.

In a climate where mixed-race individuals can be seen at best (by both blacks and whites) as able to relate to only half of the collective experience (be that experience one of struggle or of prosperity), there is a sense that they are not fully accepted by either side. In many cases, this can lead to a strong sense of ambivalence among mixed-race people. *To which side (black or white) does one affiliate? How do you strike a balance? By whom will you be fully accepted: blacks, whites or other mixed-race people?*

Obviously childhood experiences, upbringing and family background will have a great influence on how each individual answers these questions. For example, a mixed-race child who has grown up in a loving and protective all-white family environment may have been unduly sheltered from the adult realities of racism, both overt and covert, within wider society. Whereas one could argue that a mixed-race child brought up in a multicultural environment with close connections to black family members, will be better equipped to deal with such situations because of the shared experience and prior knowledge of the black family unit.

My own experience as a mixed-race woman has been slightly different to the majority due to the fact that when it comes to parentage, my mother is the black half of the partnership.

My mum was born to Jamaican parents (in Jamaica) and my dad to an Irish father and English mother in Nottinghamshire. They have been happily married since 1979. My younger sister and I are their only children, both born in the UK. I have never known anything other than the balanced influence of their continuous presence, and from both sides of the family.

Sunday afternoons for me and my sister have been a mix of driving out to drink tea in front of a real coal fire in my Irish Grandad's living-room, then travelling back home to demolish a weekly plate of rice, peas, chicken and salad at my Jamaican nana's house. It's because of this that I am knowledgeable about the Irish love of hurling, which is like hockey, Guinness and 'Danny Boy' while still being able speak patios freely, cook a serious Dutch-pot of curried goat, and sing the words of Gregory Isaacs, Bob Marley and Janet Kay when taking a musical trip down memory lane.

Looking back, I wouldn't have had it any other way. The combination of cultural influences has enriched rather than confused my childhood. Ironically, I've found that the Jamaicans and the Irish have a lot in common, historically. For example, there is their experience as post-war immigrants coming to England. Both endured the classic barriers of 'no blacks, no dogs, no Irish'. Culturally, they are two vibrant ethnic groups that embrace others.

Although not entirely unique, my experience is one of 'the minority'. After a brainstorm and scanning the many mixed-race people I knew personally, I worked out that only two others had a black mother. As women (of colour or not), it can be assumed that our mothers mainly influence us: by their examples, behaviour, stories and experiences.

In many cases, the mixed-race women I know well have been brought-up by white mothers, often without the assistance or presence of their black fathers which, in some cases, has meant no contact with any of their black family. So if perception is everything, how does society view these women who are half black, yet without a black influence?

This idea of 'how we are seen' has been particularly noticeable in our interactions with the opposite sex. The ideas they have about us, their commonly held opinions, fantasies and beliefs are all based on the issue of our 'mixed-race-ness'.

I have illustrated a selection of these situations below. This two-part list is not by any means exhaustive, more a collection of the experiences I and other mixed-race women have encountered,

Black men see us as:
Thinking we are 'too nice' because we are light-skinned and, therefore, 'superior' to darker skinned women.

This will lead us to either: play hard to get with black men or prefer to form relationships with white men (who stereotypically have the money, power and status).

We are easy (sexually) and docile (easy to seduce and control). Traits we would, presumably, have inherited from our white mothers as they were previously 'picked-up' in this way by our black fathers.

Overly keen to attach ourselves to any black man in an attempt to prove our cultural affiliation.

Lacking in any 'black' culture, most likely due to the absence of black parental influence.

'Trophy' girlfriends, but not necessarily 'wife' material.

White men see us as:
'Easier to approach,' and an alternative to 'real' black women.

'Exotic'.

'Forbidden Fruit'.

Not half white and half black, but rather not 'fully black'.

One drop theory
For me the 'one drop theory', which developed in the USA, has always been a factor in my thinking about perception and identity. The theory originally began in relation to miscegenation (the interbreeding of races) during slavery. During that period, due to frequent rapes on slave plantations for example, a number of light-skinned children were born. As time went on, there was still widespread segregation, but there were those 'Negroes' who were so pale that they could 'pass for white' and access better opportunities in this way. However in the eyes of white society, those whom we would now label as mixed-race were still classed as 'Negroes'. It was believed that once you could trace 'one drop' of black blood within your family tree, you were no longer considered white and lost any privileges.

This theory affects ideas of which cultural groups will accept a mixed-race individual as one of their own. Black communities have been historically expected to care for the mixed-races as they were 'non-white'. Nowadays, with the high rates of both teenage pregnancy and failed interracial relationships leaving unprepared white mothers to cope with mixed-race children, it seems the tables have turned. We are now seeing large numbers of mixed-race people entering adulthood after a white dominated childhood experience.

Is either experience ideal? Which one better caters for the needs of people from two separate cultures? Is it, therefore, any surprise that some view mixed-race people as culturally confused?

As neither of them are mixed-race, I know that my parents cannot honestly say they have any in-depth knowledge of my experiences, but at least they are both around to learn about them. From having girls at school feeling the need to tell me that I'm 'not black' to being reminded as a child that I am 'as much white' as I am black, I was constantly faced with the enigma of my ethnicity.

Like many, I feel that diversity should be celebrated. Everyone has the right to know about their roots, even if parents aren't around to participate in the teaching and learning process. After all, knowledge is power. On the face of things, most mixed-race people will be visually darker-skinned and/or less Eurocentric looking than Caucasians. So it's obvious upon sight to anyone who looks at you that you are not white, which inevitably leads to questions about your ethnicity.

I think there is something terribly sad about a person who knows nothing of their background and culture. Endeavour to know more. Parents of any race have a duty to teach their children about every aspect of their culture, to avoid raising a generation of clueless, randomly labelled mixed-race children, where the children themselves have no idea what the 'mix' actually is.

When people ask me: *What do you see yourself as?* Or when I hear, *But Nicki, you seem to draw more to the black side, probably because of your mum huh? Do you see yourself black?* I say, "I see myself as what I am, a woman of colour – a mixed-race female."

A final question to mixed race-women: *Do we see ourselves as women first and mixed-race second?* I do. The unique condition of our ethnicity allows us to relate, on some level, to both black and white women. We are all subject to similar sexist prejudices and share similar experiences with men, families and careers, although it cannot be denied that cultural differences can alter these also.

The problem I always had with the definition 'half-caste' was the classification of being <u>half</u> of something and therefore a <u>whole</u> of nothing. Rather than seeing 'mixed-race-ness' as being subdivisions of cultures, let's view this multiplicity as an inherent part of our being, which is an enriching factor as opposed to a detrimental one.

Has anyone ever considered that the increasing presence of mixed-race people in Britain today is teaching those on either side (black and white) that the issue of ethnicity is neither steadfast nor unwavering? We are in fact representing the modern day blurring of previously sharply drawn colour bars that brings with it a range of debatable pros and cons.

In a social climate where perception is everything, be sure to perceive yourself positively; the rest will then begin to fall into place.

BYE-BYE, BABAR
(OR: WHAT IS AN AFROPOLITAN?)

Taiye Tukali-Wosornu

It's moments to midnight on Thursday night at the Medicine Bar in London. Zak, boy-genius DJ, is spinning a Fela Kuti remix. The little downstairs dancefloor swells with smiling, sweating men and women fusing hip-hop dance moves with a funky sort of *djembe*.

The women show off enormous afros, tiny t-shirts, gaps in teeth; the men with incredible torsos unique to and common on African coastlines. The whole scene speaks of the Cultural Hybrid: kente cloth worn over low-waisted jeans; 'African Lady' over Ludacris bass lines; London meets Lagos meets Durban meets Dakar. Even the DJ is an ethnic fusion: Nigerian and Romanian, a fair, fearless leader, bobbing his head as the crowd reacts to a sample of 'Sweet Mother'.

Were you to ask any of these beautiful, brown-skinned people that basic question, "Where are you from?" you'd get no single answer from a single smiling dancer. This one lives in London but was raised in Toronto and born in Accra; that one works in Lagos but grew up in Houston, Texas. 'Home' for this lot is many things: where their parents are from; where they go for vacation; where they went to school; where they see old friends; where they live (or live this year). Like so many African young people working and living in cities around the globe, they belong to no single geography, but feel at home in many.

They (read: we) are Afropolitans – the newest generation of African emigrants, coming soon or collected already at a law firm/chem lab/jazz lounge near you. You'll know us when you see us by our funny blend of London fashion, New York jargon, African ethics, and academic successes.

Some of us are ethnic mixes (e.g. Ghanaian/Jamaican, Nigerian/

Swiss), others are merely cultural mutts: American accent, European affect and African ethos. Most of us are multilingual. In addition to English and a Romantic or two, we understand some indigenous tongue(s) and speak a few urban vernaculars.

There is at least one place on the Continent to which we tie our sense of self: be it a nation-state (Ethiopia), a city (Ibadan), or simply an auntie's kitchen. Then there's the G8 city or two (or three) that we know like the backs of our hands, and the institutions (corporate, academic) that know *us* for our focus. We are Afropolitans: not citizens, but Africans of the world.

It isn't hard to trace our genealogy. Starting in the sixties, the young, gifted and broke left Africa in pursuit of higher education and happiness abroad. A study done in 1999 estimated that between 1960 and 1975 about 27,000 highly skilled Africans left the Continent for the West.

Between 1975 and 1984, the number shot to 40,000 and then doubled again by 1987, representing about 30% of Africa's highly skilled manpower. Unsurprisingly, the most popular destinations for these emigrants included Canada, Britain and the United States, but Cold War politics produced unlikely scholarship opportunities in Eastern Bloc countries like Poland, as well.

Some three decades later, this scattered tribe of pharmacists, physicists, physicians, (and the odd polygamist) has set up camp around the globe. The caricatures are familiar. The Nigerian physics professor with faux-Coogi sweater; the Kenyan marathon runner with long legs and rolled 'Rs', the heavyset Gambian braiding hair in a house that smells of burnt Kanekalon. Even those unacquainted with synthetic extensions can conjure an image of the African immigrant with only the slightest of pop culture promptings: Eddie Murphy's "Hello, Babar."

But somewhere between the 1988 release of *Coming to America*, and the 2001 crowning of a Nigerian Miss World, the general image of young Africans in the West transmorphed from goofy to gorgeous.

Leaving out the painful question of cultural condescension in that beloved film, one wonders what happened in the years between Prince Akeem and Queen Agbani? One answer is: adolescence.

The Africans that left Africa between 1960 and 1975 had children, and most overseas. Some of us were bred on African shores then shipped to the West for higher education, others born in much colder climates and sent home for cultural re-indoctrination. Either way, we spent the eighties chasing after accolades, eating fufu at family parties, and listening to adults argue politics. By the turn of the century (the recent one), we were matching our parents in number of degrees or achieving things our 'people' in the grand sense only dreamed of.

This new demographic – dispersed across places like Brixton, Bethesda, Boston, Berlin – has come of age in the 21st century, redefining what it means to be African. Where our parents sought safety in traditional professions like medicine, law, banking and engineering, we are branching into fields like media, politics, music, venture capital and design. Nor are we shy about expressing our African influences (such as they are) in our work. Artists like Keziah Jones, *Trace* founder/editor Claude Gruzintsky, architect David Adjaye and novelist Chimamanda Achidie exemplify what Gruzintsky calls the "21st century African".

What distinguishes this lot and its like (in the West and at home) is a willingness to complicate Africa – namely, to engage with, critique, and celebrate the *parts* of Africa that mean the most to them. Perhaps what most typifies the Afropolitan consciousness is this refusal to oversimplify, the effort to understand what is ailing in Africa alongside the desire to honour what is uniquely wonderful. Rather than essentialising the geographical entity, we seek to comprehend its cultural complexity; to honour its intellectual and spiritual legacies; to sustain our parents' values.

For us, being African must *mean* something. The media's portrayals (war, hunger) won't do. Neither will the New World trope of bumbling, blue-black doctor. Most of us grew up aware of 'being from' a blighted place, of having last names linked to countries linked to lack and corruption. Few of us escaped those nasty 'booty-scratcher' epithets, and fewer still that sense of shame when visiting paternal villages. Whether we were ashamed of ourselves for not being more familiar with our parents' culture, or ashamed of that culture for not being more "advanced", can be unclear.

What *is* manifest is the extent to which the modern African adolescent is tasked to forge a sense of self from wildly disparate sources. You'd never know it looking at those dapper lawyers in global firms, but most were once supremely self-conscious of being so 'in between'. Brown-skinned without a bedrock sense of 'blackness,' on the one hand, and often teased by African family members for 'acting white' on the other – the baby-Afropolitan can get what I call "lost in transnation".

Ultimately, the Afropolitan must form an identity along three dimensions: national, racial, cultural – with subtle tensions in between. While our parents can claim single countries as home, we must *define* our relationship to the places we live; how British or American we are (or act) is, in part, a matter of affect.

Often unconsciously, and over time, we choose which bits of a national identity (from passport to pronunciation) we internalise as central to our personalities. So, too, the way we see our race – whether black or biracial or none of the above – is a question of *politics*, rather than pigment; not all of us claim to be black. Often this relates to the way we were raised, whether proximate to other brown people (e.g. black Americans) or removed. Finally, how we conceive of race will accord with where we locate ourselves in the history that produced 'blackness' and the political processes that continue to shape it.

Then there is that deep abyss of culture, ill defined at best. One must decide what comprises 'African culture' beyond filial piety and pepper soup. The project can be utterly baffling – whether one lives in an African country or not. But the process is enriching, in that it expands one's basic perspective on nation and selfhood. If nothing else, the Afropolitan knows that nothing is neatly black or white; that to 'be' anything is a matter of being sure of who you are uniquely.

To 'be' Nigerian is to belong to a passionate nation; to be Yoruba, to be heir to a spiritual depth; to be American, to ascribe to a cultural breadth; to be British, to hold the passport. That is, this is what it means *for me* – and that is the Afropolitan privilege. The acceptance of complexity common to most African cultures is not lost on her prodigals. Without that intrinsically multi-dimensional thinking, we could not make sense of ourselves.

If this sounds a little self-congratulatory – a little 'aren't-we-the-coolest-damn-people-on-earth? – I say: yes it is, necessarily. It is high time the African stood up. There is nothing perfect in this formulation. For all our Adjayes and Achidies, there is a brain drain back home. Most Afropolitans could serve Africa better *in* Africa than at the Medicine Bar on Thursdays. To be fair, a number of African professionals are returning, and there is consciousness among the ones who remain, an acute awareness among this brood of 'too-cool-for-school' that there's work to be done.

There are those among us who wonder to the point of weeping: where next, Africa? When will the scattered tribes return? When will the talent repatriate? What lifestyles await young professionals at home? How to invest in Africa's future? The prospects can seem grim at times. The answers aren't forthcoming. But if there was ever a group who could figure it out, it is this one, unafraid of the questions.

Interviews

DEBORAH AKINPELU

"My essay *Notes of a Black Woman*, was written five years ago, after reading an article in *Pride* magazine. It was about a white English lady who identified with black people, and a black lady of African heritage who identified with white people because of where she grew up. While reading the article it made me think of how I felt while growing up in Vienna, Austria.

My dad moved to Vienna in 1973. His uncle was there and the tuition was free. He planned to complete his degree and then go back to Nigeria.

My mum followed three years later. Then they had my sister and me. They always said they would go back to Nigeria, but it never happened. I've only been to Nigeria once.

The mentality in Nigeria is very different to the European mentality. Whatever I said or did, my parents would say that I was just a European girl. What did I know? I don't speak Yoruba that well, but I understand it.

I was 16 when I first came to London. I stayed for two weeks. The first thing I noticed was how at home I felt. No one was bothered whether I was black or blue. When I went to the shops, the staff smiled as they served me. I never had that experience in Vienna.

When I returned home, I cried because I had to face the staring again and have shop workers ignore me. I don't ponder on it or think about it too much. If you did, you would just get bitter.

When I started at Middlesex University, at first I didn't get on with other black girls my age. I got on with older people. I don't know why.

A lot of black girls knew each other from college so they were already friends.

I thought they spoke too fast. I didn't want to say pardon me all the time because they would think I was thick. I have lost my accent. People now think that I was born here.

One of the first places to feature my essays and poetry was the Body of Christ Ministries website three years ago. When you think of black writers you always think of black issues, but I might want to write about love without including race.

I don't see the world in black and white. When I am with my white friends I don't see myself as the black girl. I just see myself as Debbie and them as the people they are.

My favourite book is 'Battlefield of the Mind' by Joyce Meyer. It is a Christian book and it helped with the perceptions I had of myself. I now think more positively about my environment and myself.

When I was 16 I read a biography on Steve Biko. I didn't know a lot about black history at that time. He did a lot for his people and he wanted their voices to be heard. As I live my life, I want my voice to be heard as well."

DANIELLA BLECHLER

"Questions about my identity are a daily thing from black people, white people, cab drivers.

When I lived in Tanzania, East Africa, for about a year, I found that my being a mixed-race woman was beyond their thinking. They weren't even used to seeing white people. The people where I lived didn't even believe black people lived in England.

People asked where I was from. I would say my dad is Polish-English and Jewish, and my mum is Jamaican. They couldn't even take the whole Polish-English thing on board, but with Jamaica they would shout 'Bob Marley'.

It makes you feel like a breed apart sometimes. I just draw upon it as an experience. I feel like I'm a Londoner more than anything else.

Growing up in Hounslow I was surrounded by mixed-race kids. I went to a school with mainly black and Asian kids, but I had to leave because somebody got stabbed. So I was whisked away at eight to St David's, a private school in Middlesex. On my first day there I counted the number of black and Asian pupils. There were five. It was such a shock to me being in a completely different environment.

A blond-haired, blue-eyed girl came up to me and said, 'I thought this was a white school.' My innocence showed because I thought, how could you think that the uniforms were white. It didn't even click to me what she meant, but I made lots of friends.

I feel that because of my life journey, not because I'm mixed-race, I can relate to a lot of different people on different levels.

My poem *History X* is an exploration of both sides of my cultural identity. It highlights the affect and progression of these two journeys and survival, as both my parents are descendents of enslaved people.

My mother's descendants were the Maroon slaves who rebelled against the system, but despite gaining independence they signed a treaty promising to return any escaped slaves they encountered. To me, this still makes them victims of mental slavery.

My dad's family went through the Holocaust. His uncle created this website with the family tree and history. On my mother's side, it is hard to trace back as clearly. That is where the X in the title comes from. Where history is lost and has been taken away.

So many people are hell bent on looking back. I'm not saying that's a bad thing because you can't move forward unless you know where you've come from.

But some people are so backward in their thinking they don't realise that we are in 2005; that things have moved forward. The question is: what are we going to do to create history?

I've had a poem published by United Press in an anthology called 'Rhyme and Reason'. I was 22 at the time and it felt really cool. It was good to make a contribution.

I read writers such as Maya Angelou, Louise Bennett, Courttia Newland, John Irving and Alice Walker. With Maya, her journey, strength and personality shine through her writing.

I don't go out and look for books that are by mixed-race women. I look for books that appeal to me. I don't think about whether a book is reflecting a mixed-race point of view."

NICKI MURPHY

"When I decided to send in my essay *Labels,* I thought, this is giving away a part of me. They were my opinions and observations as a mixed-race woman on interracial dating. I wondered whether people were going to be offended. But as I've never been published before, despite writing at university and personally for six years, this feels really important to me.

Some black guys think that mixed-race women think they are too nice and superior because we are light-skinned.

Some black women tell me they are treated differently by their black boyfriends because they are darker skinned. One black woman said that a former boyfriend used to invite her to his house, but didn't take her out for meals or to meet his parents. Yet he did all these things with his previous girlfriends who were all light-skinned.

In my case, my mum was born in Jamaica and came over here when she was seven. My dad's parents are Irish, but he was born in England. I grew up in Nottingham.

Mixed-race women write, but they are not necessarily writing from a mixed race angle. You don't get the 'I'm writing this in my view as a mixed-race woman, through my eyes in this skin'. They write from the woman's view or the black view.

'*White Teeth*' by Zadie Smith was a big breakthrough, but it is a very multicultural book, with Asian and Turkish characters. I didn't feel like it was from the mixed-race perspective. It was the melting pot story.

In the UK you have a whole mixed-race group of people emerging. This isn't new, but we haven't been properly represented. Mixed-race is now in the census. We can tick our own box whereas before we had to pick black or white.

There is the whole thing about the 'one drop' theory: you are either black or you are not. A lot of mixed-race women frame themselves like this and by how other people see them.

I know a lot of mixed-race women who say I'm black or a woman of colour or my mum might be white, but that is her issue. Not a lot of women stand firm in their mixed-raceness.

When I go abroad I'm often mistaken for another race. In New York, so many people thought I was Latino or Hispanic. They project their assumptions onto you. By the time they figure out they are wrong they feel stupid. They are not really interested in the real answer. If they were, they would come up and ask you where you are from.

In the UK there is the strong potential for a mixed-race culture to rise up. In London particularly, it feels as if people are more willing to accept collective experiences.

My whole love affair with reading started with Maya Angelou. Her writing is very lyrical. Maya's words just flow off the page. They are inspirational because she doesn't hold back. She doesn't mind how treacherous the story is, how bad it looks or how amoral what she has done is. She just tells the truth. It is brave writing."

HYACINTH MYERS

"When I was younger I used to feel that me and my three brothers and sisters didn't fit in. The language directed towards us always made me feel odd. Names like mongrel, like you were some kind of disgusting mixture.

My mother is white English. I remember when my mum was harassed or abused in the streets while she was with us. It was really horrible, so sometimes I would never say I was mixed. Both of my sisters went through a period of thinking they were Chinese because they didn't want to be half black and half white.

Poetry has always been my escape. A lot of my poems are about love. I seem more inspired by that. I've been writing on and off since I was 13. I never wrote anything to explore what it was like to be mixed-race. So when I saw the advert for this anthology I began to write about my experiences.

My favourite poem, *Suggestions*, was written within ten minutes. It's about what a lot of mixed-raced people encounter where it is suggested that both of your parents are black.

When you make a disclosure that one of your parents is white, people are sometimes not very accepting of that reality. You are made to feel that you are less black, less pure. I now make a habit of letting people know from the beginning before any kind of friendship develops.

It's quite odd, I think, in this day and age to do that. I still don't understand why it should be an issue, but I know it is for some people.

When I was much younger, when I was doing a lot of self discovery, it felt easier not to say my mum was white. I thought it was easier to make people think that I was black. After a while I felt that I was denying a part of myself so now I just say it.

I've had around six poems published. They have been in a few anthologies by the Forward Press. A few have been published in poetry magazines.

Two years ago, when I finally showed some of my work to a very close friend, she said, 'why don't you get published?' I was really scared and said no. But then I decided to send off a few poems and the first one was published. So I've just carried on.

I like Iyanla Vanzant. She writes from her experiences and her books are so easy to read. Maya Angelou is another source of inspiration. There are quite a lot of writers I like, though I don't remember all of their names. As long as they write something inspiring that touches me at the time, I'll read it.

I don't really read a lot of poetry. I do like some of Tupac's poetry from 'The Rose that Grew from Concrete', and dub poets like Benjamin Zephaniah and Linton Kwesi-Johnson."

CINNAMON

"What's it like being us?"

Part 2

Poems

Things that make you go hmm....

Falling in love at a very young age
Every crush is a bright, blank, new page
Being in love twenty four seven
A feeling like you're in chocolate heaven

Roaming the streets without a home
Not even the luxury of a mobile phone
Lying awake thinking if there's anything to eat
Walking for food is hurting your feet

The world always seems to be at war
Surely mankind can do much, much more
Waking up and feeling fine
Praying that today you have a lot more time

Taking the life of another man
Done because he looked at you and you can
Burying a loved one before their time
Being around a man with a gun was them only crime

Shouting and screaming all of the time
Is this negative energy making you feel fine?
Handling problems well, to make you feel proud

Are you the one standing out in the crowd?

Working all hours, being rich but with no time for play
Wondering whatever had happened to the day
Leisure is pleasure, fun and laughter
Don't wait for the joy in the life ever after

Judging another by the colour of their skin
Thinking about what they've done, have they committed a sin?
The bad seeds of some men, doesn't mean all
Help them to rise and don't sneer if they fall

Living your life all on your own
No one to listen when you want a good moan
Dying alone you know the time is near
Do you have the faith so that there is less fear?

Telling those close that, "I love you"
If they were gone tomorrow what would you do?
Always being thankful for what you have got
Millions out there would appreciate your lot

Life can be difficult all in itself
Whether you are poor or you have wealth
Situations may at times seem to be all doom and gloom
But isn't there always time to make room

For the things that make you go hmmm....

Bisi Akinola

Staying Here

It is hard to imagine the old woman's
delicate frame was once so full of life:
radiant as she sashayed, the way only a
Caribbean woman can, along the main street

past the limers and diners playing hide
and seek with the fierce noon-day sun.
How she loved to laugh.
How she loved to run and dance …

but now? Now, she can barely stand as
her slow, slippered feet shuffle along the
aloof, charcoal coloured pavement.
She's leaning heavily on the arm of her

youngest grandson. I cannot see her face
only the back of her head covered with
handfuls of short, cotton wool plaits.
What is she still doing here?

She should be living out her twilight years
'back home' wherever that might be; not here
in the Mother Country with the changeable
climate that has transformed silky, smooth,

dark chocolate skin into an ashen shell;
the unforgiving north winds that grip her
joints in a stranglehold so severe she
cries sometimes from the pain. Perhaps it

---

was her decision to remain here, but
I cannot help wondering whether she
would be so frail, so fragile had she
returned home to the sun.

Tania Charles

Grandad

For as long as I can remember,

Pictured his smile in mine;
Where my full eyes came from.

The bus will take an hour; then
Ten minutes to climb
The long gritty hill,
Cooked in Jamaican heat.

Sat tight in cramped container
Its tyres pretend to take strain.

Weighed down by shiny limbed
School children, full-bodied women in
Spangled blouses, elders in straw hats
Shielding squinting eyes.

I smile as elbows and bottoms stick in
Unsuspecting faces,
Trying to find some balance.

I turn.
Framed through cracked window
I see my Grandad,
Waiting to cross the street.

I know that's him...definitely is him.
Same features as mummy,
Same posture as me.

No one can tell me different.
It's him alright –
From the one photo I've seen:

I—Just—**Know.**

My cousin insists I didn't see him.
Couldn't possibly know how he looks
From one, single photo.

Trust me.
I grab her hand; we get off at the
Next stop.

We run as fast
As Jamaican heat and humidity will allow
Legs to pump
And chests to heave.

We get nearer to the old man
In white shirt,
Chest high grey slacks
And trilby.

"Grandad?" "Grandad!"

The elder turns.
His face matches mine.
He looks on *bemused*. Then amused.

My crumpled baby picture
Drawn from his wallet –
His smile, broad, as he
Enfolds my teenage frame.

Holding, squeezing, dispelling
Years of family tears;
Distance.

My visit…
Also yearned.

Patricia Foster

Resolution

With slack legs crossed and shallow breath, I sit cushioned between
your Wedgwood thighs, drunk on the smell of your late summer skin

"Lean in," you breeze through the lock of my hair as I dare to lift my
   head to see,
Me, crumpled and curled among you,
You, soothing oils into the belly of your palm, until I'm charmed.

Defenceless and humbled by the rhythm of your majesty
Each touch renews my need to be. Here.
So I stay, as braids coil east then I bow west

And you trace the folds of these ears, follow the curve of this
   docile neck
And then capture the fall of my crown.

Louise Hercules

Abandon

How can you desert your own blood?
Your flesh, your genes?
Is it easier to give up completely?
When it's a voiceless baby?
A crawling toddler unable to question, *"Why me?"*

Why ditch me? – innocent and needing
Your fatherly love, your guidance, your reassurance.
Someone to mirror my image,
Someone who looked like me, my colour tones,
My history is wrapped up in your skin and your bones.

Dumping your child, trying much later
In my ninth year to reclaim me;
But your plans were never materialised
Through strong 'protective' grandmother intervention
The best laid plans......

In my twenty-third year I found you
Only after the secret of your attempt to see me
Was revealed; I found you – easily.
So why did it take you so long
To find me?

And in the most difficult year of my life
1988, my thirty-fifth year – You abandon me again
– This time with no intention of reclaiming, or renewing.
And all for ancestral and cultural sunny climes
For marital bliss once again.

Migration brought you here – this
Motherland; here you had three children
I discover this in my twenty-third year.
Only it is too late, too bloody late for us to
Make those blood ties really work

Too late for my younger brother who passed in his sixth-year.
Too late for my younger sister, an Italian/Guyanese mixture
Who cannot even give voice to her experiences of you.
Our voices are unique, fragmented
Living close, but miles of landscape barricade our feelings and
thoughts.

Nicole Moore

Dedication

At 5 foot 5 she's a giant: personality, passion, presence
belittles many
Her humour is ageless, her laughter, contagious
Her kindness is unselfishly abundant.

She's wise, her school was life, 'The Ruthless Teacher'
Mother, woman, friend, you'd have to travel far and wide
To find her equal: she stands alone

Never a stranger to hard work, she brought six lives into the world
Lifting us up with strong hands, and setting us on the path to life

She taught us well, with lessons from life:
Right from wrong, good from bad
Respect and compassion for our fellow man,
I don't think we understood at the time

She opened her heart and her home
There were many occasions, when strangers were seated at
  our table
Sharing the best of what we had, always leaving with bags filled
With food and clothes for days to come

Even when times were hard, she rolled up her sleeves and
  persevered
Courage and resourcefulness, always saved the day
She wasted little energy pondering on the pain, disappointment
And sadness that often weighed her down

When I was a child, I knew little about her sacrifice

Even as a teenager, it was always there and yet,
I took her sacrifice for granted
It wasn't until I could reason as an outsider looking in:
That I could appreciate that her sacrifice, was another name for love

Mother, thank you for your sacrifice
For there were times along the way when I believed
You were doing me far from good

Now I see you for the fine human being that you are
And I beam with pride
For now I realise, what I am, what I hope to be...
Is all thanks to you.

Karen Plumb

Gender
Black Brother

I see you and want to meet you, but the way you stand and twinkle your eyes, makes me wonder if you're looking at another who's passing you by.

Another? Another? Another?

I hopefully pray that another person does not need to portray to you what I have in store.
Love not war.
The glory, perchance!

I stand, I stare, I weigh up and bear but black brother, how can I show you, I want to get closer to you.
Black brother you're so strong.
I don't want to make a wrong move.
Bro' you do not know how you're making me crave your attention.
I yearn for a moment, a glance, or a conversation…

Every time I see you, I ask myself what can I do to make you see that you deserve me.
I look at your strong stature and lose myself in the thought of any physical contact.
I see your warm seductive eyes soothing me, like a pleasant daydream that refuses to end.
Your eyes don't tell any lies, I see the pain when you look into my eyes.
I see the pain that rains, the pain that pours, and the pain that resists your need to explore.

When I see you.
I am tongue-tied trying to hide my feelings, which are my only guide...
Black bro' you have no clue, that I analysed you the moment
  you said, "Hi boo."
But I am so shy because you are the professional I don't want to
  pass me by...
I will take my time to make the right move; I hope you're ready
  to finally choose this woman

Time is ticking on.
Black brother you don't see this woman is expressing intellectually?
I am scared you won't feel my vibe, my charm my alarm...
Scared you'll be, snapped up, before you meet my arms...
But I know, who I am and what I want,
If I don't get you, there is no need for me to front...

Black bro' you're looking smoother.... feeling livelier.
Taking time out to make a move....
I like your style.
Ready to convince me that you're worth my while.
I see you're not leaving me hanging or dragging behind your every wish.
I acknowledge, you're willing to take a chance.
I see you're real and that is a big deal.

I am aware you have taken time to challenge what ifs?
Flashing lights make me want to scream in delight.
I search...
The time has come to reveal my dream.
The streams surge.
I urge...

Iesha Slater

Brown Eyes

Race is a race

Race is a race
To be strong enough
To represent enough
To be a part of when needed and a partner of when not.

Black race! known as the burden race.
A need to chase... A need to fit in...
We need to change the domination of the ongoing circle.
Forget the rat race and forget the black race ever being a burden.
The black race is Ace.
We all go through hard times.
But nothing can take away our gifted minds.

Our in-depth ancestry
That paved the way
Our ancestors would be hurt to see their hard work and lives to be
    in vain!
Black on black crime shows the strain that we can't get along
What's wrong, why have we stopped communicating?

We are a liability to ourselves, when we walk away from our dreams.
Black race is a part of us, nobody else.
Why do we struggle to win the race, when we have arrived?
Somehow forgotten to turn around and help another black face.
Not all need help but many do.
It would be a shame to reign in vain
It would be a great loss to alter a wound without fixing it.

We are one!
Our precious vibe
Our precious talents

Our personalities of delight
Our skills
Our laughter
Our warmth
Our voice
Our attitude
Our strength
Our culture
Our Oneness

When will we realise we need to relate.
Not Escape
Enjoy our lives
Make sense of our opportunities
And breathe…

Iesha Slater

Endless Brown

Endless brown
Curves so round
Round eyes brown
Looking down
Down on you
Down on me
Down on skin
As smooth as can be
Smooth soft lips
Chocolate rippled hips
Creamy thighs creamed
Cocoa butter slick
Butter would melt
Legs toned svelte
Tone it to perfection
Oh my what a complexion
Take a black coffee
And splash it with milk
Pile mahogany wood
On top of white silk
Mix it up and stir it well
Pour it down on me
In one enchanting spell
Spell me a word
That never ends
Enchant my skin
That's the same
More or less
One for a thousand and one reasons
Not to frown

When you're gazing down
On your beautiful Endless brown,

Ony Uhiara

Brown Eyes

This Red Earth

This Coconut tree, this country that's not quite as sweet as the
Mango my Auntie offered me.
Carefree, I lick the juice from my wrists, not quite so free to care;
There's a price and there's a twist.
The neighbourhood hoodlum dons the hood of his hoody,
Hiding his unwashable shame. Still, I'm glad I came.
   Look closer, much closer, it's not all the same;
I wonder how I'd survive this part of life's game?
The street-side selling, the roads ever swelling
With fuel deprived fighters, strugglers, wishful thinkers.
The motorcycle taxi action,
The education that's just not happening,
The government walls with all the cracks in;
You know it's never gonna change.
   Nigerian breath on a butterfly's wing,
How sweet it is to hear Mama sing.
Oya, come let's go,
Why are you making this ride so slow?
I've got beautiful cousins waiting to show
Me how a Nigerian girl's life might go
If she was living in Nigeria.
But she won't see, how can she see it yet?
Until she's living in the very depths of
her bloodline's village.
Adopting the ways in which customs are set.
Aspects of London life she'd have to forget.
   But this is all just to speculate,
"What if my life was woven with
Different threads of fate?"

Ony Uhiara

Snapshots: Once upon a time in Nigeria...

There was a butterfly in the green,
My blue bum – you caught that one
And me hitting you and the lads were there.
There was the sea
And the sky whizzing past.
There was you in the landscape,
You swearing- I caught that one
And me in the landscape- maybe
With a motor bike
There was him and me
And something on the ground.
My flowering hand.
There was your hand and a ring.
Me, the chicken and you
Then there was palm wine sunshine,
Oh, there was you smiling at me
And I think the lads were there.
There was him and you -
I definitely caught that one.
Then there was him, me, you and him.
The mango tree and you.
Yeah, then there was you and me sitting-
Partly reflected after last night's storm.
There was you, me and him.
Now, there was you, mum, baby and me.
There was me clinging to you and
The lads of course were there too.
And there was him, the car and you –
I caught that one also.

Ony Uhiara

The Power of a Woman

So powerful is she,
Her wonder, her style, her grace,
The beauty of a woman,
Her rhythm, her poise, her shake,
As she strides confidently,
Breaking walls, enriched with faith,
Woman…. black woman,
I see the ripples you create.

Like a picture perfect painting,
She absorbs the blank, and exudes colour,
She's performing, She's transforming,
The play of life that's set before her, She expels the ugly, and creates
the greats, For she's the shaker of her destiny, Woman black woman,
A work of art God made impressively.

Your beauty, au-naturel,
Seeps through each planted struggle,
Causing the paths your feet have travelled,
To unleash from your soles rose petals,
The very smile on your face, Can transform old things into new,
Woman black woman,

I see God's beauty within you.

Lynda Wireko

Essays

BLONDE-HAIRED, BLUE-EYED JESUS

Martha Matthews

I wanna look like Jesus.

Everything good, highly rated and worthy looks like Jesus, especially on TV. Everyone else is a criminal, a clown or on the US Olympic team. The better quality black characters invariably get shot first while the others are embarrassing caricatures.

A big dark man stole from a pale passer-by.

The neighbour's neighbour is a laughing stock as his music, clothes and hair are all too loud.

I wanna look like the person I pray to.

Our Father
Which art in Heaven
Hallowed be Thy name

My friend's hair is so easy to comb. I spend the bulk of morning playtime with her hairbrush. I imagine that she doesn't get her knuckles conked as she doesn't have to put her hand in her head to relieve the pain of the parting, plaiting and greasing of the scalp. Isabel puts her hair behind her ears, and it actually stays there!

Thy kingdom come
Thy will be done
On earth as it is in Heaven

After a hard day's learning, I would rush home from school into the arms of my family. My sister and I would put ponchos over our plaits and the two of us would prance around our bedroom flicking and swishing our manes. We would speak loudly and gesticulate wildly, walking down an imaginary catwalk in our homemade adverts.

Jen would take a wad of hair and stick it behind her ears. I would laugh and tilt my head forward, then backwards, hard. We would even stick our blue and white hair out of the windows and scream, "Rapunzel, Rapunzel, let down your hair!" It was a weird and exhilarating experience.

The dolls in my house came in a range of pink, cream and yellowish hues. There was the one that chuckled, one that wet itself and the ones that came apart too easily. Each brushstroke of their silky tresses confirmed the ugliness of my own hair, and when I turned to the red-haired rag doll or the golliwog, they only deepened my already negative thoughts.

Now and again those dolls would form part of my imaginary social arena. In true form, rag doll and golliwog were the bad guys, setting themselves upon the poor helpless pale ones. I would often end up throwing them across the room or do a mock reprimand in true schoolteacher fashion. Given the choice, who wanted to emulate a woolly-haired rag doll when you could emulate Barbie?

Give us this day
Our daily bread
And forgive us our trespasses
As we forgive those who trespass
Against us

It was decided. When I'm 14, I'm going to get my hair relaxed. Give it a good old rest. The conscious reason was because it would be easier to handle. I was gonna make myself look on earth as he does in Heaven. Get it all straight and easy to comb.

Hopefully, it will grow and I can get me a fringe and a ponytail.

I could bite my split ends while I concentrated or looked at boys. I could finger each silky strand while waiting at a bus stop or speaking on the phone. At the very least I wanted some shine. My hair was such a dusty, dull brown colour, not even proper black.

And lead us not
Into temptation

So I sit in a seat at the hairdressers. Well, my friend's seat. Her mum was the real hairdresser. I let her transform nature's delight into dead straight strands that sit on my head like wet string on a gravestone. But this was real pleasure, real love. No more plaits. No more pain. No more incessant greasing of the scalp. I could not keep my hands from my head as my fingers witnessed the texture and the release from the coil. Fair enough it burned hard as my head was not used to that kind of chemical pain, but it was a fair exchange. One that would deem me 'worth it' too!

But deliver us from evil

I knew nothing about the power of nine back then. Knew nothing of the theory about black hair and melanin. That the curl of our hair resembled the number nine, the magic number. Spirituality! Divinity! Nine, like the school child just starting out. Nine, clinging to the line. A big bold nine like the handwriting of a veteran. All different shapes and fuzzy sizes. Hair that bounces: 999 – emergency digits. Nine: ether. Didn't know that Jesus was described as having hair like wool and skin the colour of brass in that very same Bible.

And lead us not into temptation
For his name sake

The police killed a big dark man.

"Shouldn't have got himself arrested," old man Charlie said.

They got away with it, the police. It was nothing unlawful. Groups of them turn on themselves and on each other. It was given a name. Black on black crime. Never heard of blue-eyed on blue-eyed crime. Seems weird.

When Mrs Thatcher comes into power all black people have to go back 'home'. I can't tell my friends *exactly* where I'll be going as my father is a Bajan and my mother is a Trini. I haven't been to either country.

When mum was going to both places I offered to buy her some batteries.

"What for?" she asked.

"For your torch, in case the batteries run out."

"Why I need a torch?" She seemed puzzled.

"For the caves mum!" How could she forget?

"There's no caves girl. We have cities and towns and electricity, just like here."

"Ooohh!" I was genuinely surprised.

Tarzan had me believe it was all jungles, whooping and yelping where the 'dark ones' dwelled. School history books had me believe that they never existed at all during major points in history and that they were wild, an entity to be avoided and that they all ate out of one big steaming pot.

"Towns and cities huh?"

I'm gonna miss Isabel so much.

I'm gonna study hard and hopefully my teacher will realise I *should* be in the top English group. I doubt if I'll go to university or anything like that, but I definitely won't speak like mum. I'll say film, not FLim; postal order not postal ARDa; cardigan, not CADDIgan.

Do you think if my hair grows and I walk the walk and talk the talk I will be more in his image, in the Saviour's likeness? Do you think people will notice? Do you think I could pass for a blue-eyed, blonde-haired Jesus?

For thine is *the kingdom, the power and the glory, for ever and ever....*

Amen.

REVOLUTIONARY GLAMOUR

Lisa Maynard-Atem

Black style is now global: a 'lucrative' phenomenon that has revolutionised and pushed the boundaries of fashion and popular culture worldwide. Many of the trends we see today have been influenced by black culture.

It is ironic, when you consider that 50 years ago this would have been an unimaginable feat. It is testament to the fact that despite living in a world where racial prejudice remains a constant, we have been successful in breaking down some of these barriers and having a positive influence on those around us. The year 2004 was of particular significance with the V&A's exhibition. The first of its kind in the UK, it took us on a journey through Black British style over the last 50 years, from the migration of black people to the UK to the influence of garage and urban grime music in the present day: an amazing insight into the evolution of our unique style.

As a black woman, the way I look and dress has always been about more than sheer 'vanity'. For me, it is an affirmation of my individuality, a representation of my cultural background. There is history behind every piece of my attire.

Black style, generally, has many connotations. It signifies the struggle for equality, respect and freedom. The Black British dress sense represents not only the struggles that we have encountered, but the diversity of the country and, to a degree, the UK-style.

Black style is not just about the way we dress. It embodies our attitude, taste in music, gestures and language. Historically, we have been oppressed in practically every aspect of our lives. How we have chosen to adorn our bodies was the only exception and, understandably, grew in importance and became a way to show defiance against our oppressors.

Our dress sense (historically as well as currently) evolves according to particular points in time. In the 1970s, for example, the afro was a political statement, a style that evolved in response to that moment in time. Black people who came to this country in the 1950s arrived in their best clothes. This was their way of putting their best foot forward, presenting themselves (and their culture) to their new environment in a positive way. What more effective way to introduce oneself to one's new neighbours.

It's not merely the clothes you choose to wear, but the passion behind them. Anyone can put on an outfit, but to achieve the overall 'black' sense of style there has to be some substance to the clothes. They must tell the story of you, the individual.

Even clothes from mainstream 'high street' stores are being given a sense of individualism through our styles. This is what we do well. Take the tracksuit. This basic leisure outfit has been adopted into black culture, becoming symbolic of the hip-hop genre – Run DMC adopted the tracksuit and made it the mainstay of their image in the eighties and it was revived in this century.

The mention of Run DMC leads me to an area of our heritage that cannot possibly go without being mentioned – music. Black music and fashion has always gone hand in glove. But historically, it's our music that has had, and continues to have, a tremendous and overwhelming influence internationally. Leading musicians such as Elvis Presley, the 'King of Rock 'n' Roll', was greatly influenced by black music.

In the 1950s, racial prejudice was at an all time high. We were treated as second-class citizens and black musicians faced a far greater struggle for acceptance. Despite such opposition, their talent spoke for itself, and they gained recognition through their music.

These 'musical innovators' such as Billie Holiday were able to rise above the ignorance and intolerance to make others sit up and listen. In doing so, they laid the foundations for all the musicians that have subsequently followed them. From the icons of Motown to Rappers Delight to Public Enemy to Miss Dynamite; our ability to express ourselves through song is of great cultural significance. It's from music that Black British style has taken its cue, proving influential and giving a different perspective and insight into our way of life.

People outside our culture often heap various stereotypes upon the way we dress, which is frustrating, because these stereotypes are indicative of ignorance and a lack of understanding of our history and heritage. The timing of the V&A's exhibition was perfect for two reasons. Firstly, it came at a point when Black British culture is at its most influential. Secondly, the world has, once again, become a place of great unrest and tension.

Confrontation between people of different cultures has become intense. We are witnessing behaviour that is breaking bridges rather than building them. The exhibition built bridges (although small) and greater awareness of our immediate environment. The rest of the world: sit up and take note.

As a people, this 'cultural birth' has given us a power that we never had before. We should use it wisely because it can only aid our fight for acceptance and equality.

There are still many people in the world whose minds are closed to the possibility of anything different. If something as simple as clothing can help to break down more barriers, then that is something that we must seize upon.

As for black culture and style in the UK today, all I have to say in the words of Dizzee Rascal... 'fix up' and continue to 'look sharp'.

IS BLACK LOVE DEAD?

Taiye Tuakli-Wosornu

It's 10am in Brixton Market: babies crying, vendors selling, plantain frying, light rain falling, soukous in the air. People – shopping, buying, moving – crowd the space and give it life. They're *black* people mainly, en masse and in motion, a million and one shades of brown.

Two moving among the many catch my eye: a man and boy – the man about 6ft 6in with locs, the boy with cane-rowed hair. In a single stroke the man scoops up the boy and hoists him onto his sinewy shoulders. The boy laughs with delight as his gentle giant runs over the road to the tube.

Watching from under a newsagent's awning, I'm struck by the beauty of what I've just seen: black father and son in a moment of joy, pure and simple, an intimate instant. It's only after I've watched them go, and the cane-rowed head has bobbed out of sight, that I realise what caught my eye in the first place: the *rarity* of the pair. When was the last time I'd seen a black father bounce his black son on his shoulders like that? Better yet, when was the last time I'd seen a 'black father'?

Oh, that's right – in Wembley.

But this one was walking with a wan little blond woman, as was the black man I'd seen before him. In fact, *most* of the black men I see around London have white partners and/or mixed-race children. When black fathers are absent, these newly ubiquitous babies betray their patrilineal hue: caramel kids on the arms of white women or peeking from prams: unexpected.

If the father is there he will glance away warily, lagging just ever so slightly behind, with that odd combination of braggadocio and sheepishness — *yeah, that's my child* — when he does meet my eye.

Is Black Love Dead?

The standard 'pro-black' platform would posit that men like these have abandoned the race; that black men with white partners manifest a self-loathing in their lust for blond hair and blue eyes. The more psychoanalytic objector would question what it says about black men's esteem that they'd rather have children who don't bear their features than be with black partners who do.

What does it say about black men's opinions of their sisters and mothers, their view of *themselves*, that so many are choosing white women, Asian women, anything but a black woman, to mother their kids?

But what about the kids? There is something about the *look* of mixed-race children that arrests the eye. Even someone as fed up as I am with media's 'multicultural' fetish can see that. A friend of African/American/ Indian/French extraction is fond of saying: "The more you mix it, the better you make it." And I've often wondered.

From the vantage point of history, it would seem a sort of triumph that the racial lines so long employed to subjugate are blurring. In this light, mixed-race children represent a kind of moving on, their loveliness a tribute to the feat of integration.

After all, it's a slippery slope that begins with the stipulation that races shouldn't mix. European racists popularised that prohibition, along with the notion of race itself. Obviously, some black people end up with their non-black partners out of love (my African-American stepfather and his Caucasian wife, for example).

Other black people avoid their own out of a sense that their own undervalues *them*. Told they're not affluent/attractive/authentic enough, they peddle their wares elsewhere.

Then, there's the case for pure demographics, cited by professionals, students, celebrities: in certain circles the number of suitable black suitors is proscriptively low.

All of which leaves a neo-revolutionary like me in a bit of a bind.

What to paint on my picket placards? BLACK MEN FOR BLACK WOMEN! VIVA BLACK LOVE! Where to march — in Brixton Market? Who's the opposition? How to express my deep dismay at the rare sight of black fathers and children; at the number of black people choosing white partners (50% of British-born black men), without sounding racist? How to express my genuine sadness at seeing Black Love lose its mandate and base — without buying into the knee-jerk jingoism that says BLACKS MUST DATE BLACKS?

The short answer is it's not (just) about the relationships. The problem (and there *is* one) isn't only *that* we're dating whites, but *why*. And why *so many* of us feel the need, of late. I tend to think of this predominance as symptomatic of a larger ill: the dissolution of Black Peoplehood.

It Takes A Village, People

Welcome to Anthropology for Dummies. Our subject today is the Village. In its most basic sense the Village expresses the collective functioning of 'a people'. At least two institutions shape the ideal-type Village: the apprenticeship and marriage.

The practice of apprenticeship advances Village industry, while marriage (and/or procreation) sustains the population. For young men and women growing up in this Village, both practices lay a foundation of sorts: apprenticeship will channel them into various vocations, while marriage will secure their new homes. The older Villagers will take an active role in this by helping the young choose good partners and good professions; they ensure the good health of the *people*.

In modern times the notion of 'a people' has lost its relevance, but the functioning of 'the Village' in this basic sense has not. Ethnic groups in the UK (and US) view marriage as a means to collective improvement, hence Asian and Jewish mothers fussing over whom their daughters wed.

Social groups like the upper class, still use apprenticeship to advance their own, hence my wealthy classmates from Oxford using their fathers' connections to get their first jobs. From Asian grocers employing their nephews to Oxbridge debs dating family friends, there are people in London still *acting* like 'a people'.

We are not. Black people, quite simply put, no longer practice Peoplehood (or are giving up the habit more and more each passing day). In ever increasing numbers, we don't date each other, trust each other, marry each other, hire each other. We don't sustain our Village.

Men (who traditionally perpetuate a people) and women (who traditionally sustain a culture) are defecting from the project in favour of partnerships with whites. My concern is not that we date other races – clearly we're entitled to love whom we choose – but there's a critical distinction between dating because you love someone and dating because you *don't* love yourself.

My Nigerian uncle is teaching his white wife Yoruba, as he has done with their kids. In his marriage he continues to affirm our culture, our Village (as does she). By contrast, a Ghanaian cousin who dates white men in the expressed hope of having "light-eyed kids" rejects what is beautiful in African people, in search of 'enlight-skin-ment.'

Things appear no better in the realm of 'Village industry', where black professionals rarely take on (or seek out) black apprentices. Half of us appear to operate with a 'last one in, shut the door' mentality – getting our jobs then turning a blind eye to the hiring and advancement of 'us.' Meanwhile, as other groups engage in what I like to call Ethno-nepotism, we operate on the assumption that white businesses are more professional and legitimate than ours. Absent the promotion of black professionals, the patronage of black business, the pairing of black paramours and what is left of Black Peoplehood but RBG (Red, Black and Green – the colours of the African Liberation flag), and a bass beat.

The 'people' are in exodus. The Village is falling to pieces. And as it falls, I wonder if some of us aren't throwing bricks as we flee. When we have concurred with the dominant culture that straight hair and light eyes epitomise beauty; when we hesitate to invest in (our own) urban businesses; when the youth have abandoned respect for adults, are we not razing the Village on *purpose*? Is ruin an outcome or goal?

I ask, because some of us seem not to *want* to be Villagers — that is, not to be black — anymore. It's a logical goal for those who view the 'Village' as 'ghetto', and 'blackness' as 'lack'. I'm thinking of black women masking their features and culture, loath to pass both to their kids; of black men esteeming white partners as symbols of status, or opportunity.

It says something unsettling about British society that whiteness remains an access pass; that a black man on the arm of a white man or woman feels more entitled to privilege. But it says something tragic about black self-opinion that some of us, understandably tired of strife, see blackness *only* as disadvantage, nature's injustice, no more than that. For these Village expatriates, black is less: black business (less business), black beauty (less beautiful). In the boardroom or bedroom, 'black' is a thing to be shed at one's earliest opportunity.

The irony (or the tragedy) is killing us. The very same blackness we're throwing away is the Western world's number one export. Our style of dress, our limber limbs, our music, its vernacular; all are in perpetually hot demand by universal markets. I'd be the first to object to the objectification of black men and women for mass consumption, but hardly the last to question why we can't see our true worth. The issue isn't whether we are free to date 'outside' the race, but how we (mis)understand that race, its legacy and its power.

Which brings me to that tricky, tricky question: what is meant by 'black'? To speak of dating 'outside the race' implies that would-be lovers lay '*in*side the race'. But who are they or how are they defined?

If a 'black man' has a partner who is Cuban-British and chocolate brown, or Chinese-Jamaican with bone straight hair, does he fall into the 50%? That friend of mine ("the more you mix it"), what is she? *She'd* say she's black. But with creamy skin and squiggly hair, she's often told she's not ("not really").

Who *is* 'really black' in Britain? Haitians? Jamaicans? Cape Verdeans? Me? My father is Ewe (100%) but my mother an Egba/Glaswegian blend. I'm often told that I don't 'look African' and, more absurdly, that I don't 'talk black'.

If black love is dead, then 'black' must have lived — but what has it meant and what does it mean?

The Loveliness of Blackness

Now, there is, as we know, no scientific basis for human classifications of race. 'Blackness' was long ago given away as an expedient social construct. The people we call 'black' today are, in fact, the polylithic progeny of Africans, Indians, Asians, Europeans, depending on where in the world you find them.

Sharp, progressive scholarship has debunked the myth of racial type, exposed the roots of scientific racism, troubled the notion of 'race.' The trouble is, to say that black is a social construct (and stamp it INVALID for speaking of us) can obscure the ways in which blackness has moulded a culture, a people and a past.

All brown-skinned folk are *not* the same. From Bajan to Batswana to Burkinabé, we speak different languages; live different lives, develop in different contexts. We nevertheless share certain features: origins in Africa, years of oppression, but above all the habit of forming, in contexts of hardship, cultures of strength. If 'black' was wrongly applied to a people (let's call them the people of the African Diaspora), it has also denoted the brutalities they suffered as well as the cultures they formed in response.

I'm all for the rejection of language and thinking that binds us to hardship (what *révolutionnaire* isn't?). But we might be throwing out the baby of black culture with the bathwater of black oppression. The badge of blackness was *given* to us – be we Bajan, Batswana, Burkinabé – we were *given* conditions of slavery, colonialism, economic disenfranchisement, hunger. But we *created*, under these conditions of blackness, the cultures of blackness that now span the globe. In Bridgetown, Gaborone, Ouagadougou, 'black culture' *is*, and has always been, real.

Africans of the Diaspora have done with 'black' what we do with everything: transforming that which is devalued by a dominant culture into something vibrant and strong. Just look at our cooking: *kontomire*, soul food – the remnants of industrial farming remixed. The ingenuity common to 'black people' is unique, in the history of the world. To look at the condition (social, historical) and define it by hardship and wanting and strife is to misunderstand what we've *made* out of blackness: the most triumphant culture on earth.

The problem (and it's a big one) isn't whom we date, but what we know or what we *don't* know/read/learn/tell our kids about our 'people'. Nor is it the case that these kids can somehow transcend being (treated as) black. Even mixed-race children (and professionals, celebrities) can run into contemporary racism.

If all our children know of 'being black' is what they learn on London streets (where women clutch their purses when they pass, or store clerks watch them shop), *we* are to be faulted for not teaching them the rest. If they *knew* that the West tried to steal then destroy us, succeeding only in making us make more of life; *knew* that we set on metropolis margins the cultural trends that world masses adore; *knew* that we're heroes, survivors, inventors, ingenious – by very definition, per force – wouldn't they love being part of this 'people'?

Wouldn't we love being black?

It's 10:02 in Brixton Market

One man shelters his son from the rain. With his looks he could come from anywhere warmer: Accra, Dakar, Negril. How he got to Lambeth, London – waiting, wet, on a Brixton street – is anyone's guess. To work? To study? Send money back home? To *eat*? There must be pain and wanting here, some measure of hardship, exhaustion or fatigue.

Despite its recent run-in with gentrification, Brixton *works*.

But there is also *movement* here, the pulse of a people who won't stay down. They're hard and hopeful, joyful people, pressing through the rain. Babies sleep in mothers' *wrappas*; vendors sell to feed their kids; soukous plays, infectiously cheerful; people work and laugh and live.

One of them, a Village elder, white-haired, waves a woman down. She smiles wide in recognition, laughing like my auntie. Despite the load he must carry, a father settles his son on his shoulders. The little boy's laughter floats through the air. These are black people.

What's not to love?

Interview

SHEREE MACK

"I hadn't revisited my autobiographical essay *Black Britain* since I first wrote it. But when I decided to put it forward for this anthology I knew I had to.

In the past I've always said I was Afro-Caribbean, but in the last few months — through my work and talking with people — I am now comfortable using the term Black British. I'd like to get to the point where I can say I'm British with no qualification.

The first thing I wrote was a poem called *Hollow* about my mum's death five years ago, and a short monologue about a young fat girl who picks up a man. She waits for what would be their first date, but he never turns up.

I was published for the first time in March 2004. I won a short story writing competition held by Brown Skin Books — erotic fiction for brown-skinned women. I won £500 and had my story published in their '*Hot Chocolate*' anthology.

Winning the competition came at a very good time because I had just given up full time teaching — I was a secondary school English teacher — and I had started on my career as a writer. It was a seal of approval that somebody else thought I could write.

My dad was from Port of Spain in Trinidad, and my mum was born in Newcastle of two mixed-race parents. My maternal grandmother was Newcastle-born to a white mother and a father from the Gold Coast. My mum's father was born in Bradford and his father was from Barbados.

I grew up in a totally white society. My family and me live in a rural village in Newcastle-upon-Tyne. We are the only black family around for miles. This has been a generational thing.

A different voice comes out of the northern region as compared to the south. There aren't a lot of black artists writing in the north because it is still viewed as a middle class activity, an intellectual thing. I didn't know black female writing existed until I was 15 and came across Toni Morrison's '*The Bluest Eye*'. When I went to university I found Joan Riley from the British context. Now it's Jackie Kay's poetry and Alice Walker's creativity. Alice makes me feel it is okay to touch on taboo subjects such as sex.

It's a constant search to find other Black British women writers, which is why I'm studying for a PhD on Black British Women Contemporary Poets. I want to know the field that I'm going into. These women write extensively, but not many have their own collections published. Most of their poems appear in anthologies.

I'm on a journey for my identity. When I was younger I was called a paki. When I went to university, because I'm not very dark, I was classed as mixed-race. Now I get asked, 'where do you come from?'

It does anger me. People seem to think they have a right to ask these questions about my race. It's like they can't get past it."

WALNUT

"You don't
sound/look/act black"

Differences

'Where's the snooty girl from head office?'
Her words ricocheted off the walls
slapping me across the face,
leaving me slightly bruised.

'If you're referring to me, I'm still here!'
My words flat-lined.
She's not so gobby now.

She's going to have to dig real deep
to get herself out of this and she won't
get far with those long, acrylic nails.

What had I done to deserve that?
I racked by brains for a reason.

On previous visits my 'sista' and I
had chatted about this and that,
we'd had a laugh and a giggle
so where the hell did *that* come from?

Am I just too quiet for her,
too reserved? Had that unnerved her?

Or maybe it's because I don't dress
and talk like Ms Black London?

Years ago I almost KO'd a black
girl at a wedding reception when she
asked me what I was into.

I left her totally dazed and confused
when I told her I didn't like
pubs, clubs or parties.

The revelation proved too much for her:
'What! You're black and don't like parties!'

Am I missing something here?

Is there some mythical handbook
the midwife forgot to give me like *The
Black Woman's Code of Conduct – A Guide*?

Why can't people take me as they find me?

Why should I have to subscribe to other
people's preconceived ideas about
what a black woman should/shouldn't do?
Does being different make me any less black?

Tania Charles

You say my love ain't political

I cross blue lines daily for you
then try not to break
when your mother
tells her friends
I'm pretty
like Cleo Laine
classy
like Lena Horne
I could be
Egyptian Israeli Italian Greek
in other words
I can pass
for something other
than what I am

I talk myself
out of toffee coloured babies
leave the womb repeatedly
around 5am to see your smile
navigate & translate
'black' spaces
into non-threatening
lexicon and hold
my secret name
under my tongue

and you say my love ain't political

Kimberly Trusty

Essays

SELF-IMAGE IS EVERYTHING...

Nicole Moore

"A positive, healthy sense of self-value and worth is the foundation of our happiness and success. When we know who we are and believe it, our greatest dreams are possible. When we doubt ourselves, question our worth, and undermine our self-value, our greatest victory will be worthless. Affirm "I am my greatest hero". That is really where it starts. We must believe in who we are and what we do. We must look up to and trust ourselves to make it through the difficulties knowing that we can. Only we can truly appreciate and celebrate our own success. We are equipped and capable of getting to where we want to be. If we have any doubts, we can always hold our own hand."

'Acts of Faith Daily Meditations for People of Color', Iyanla Vanzant

We live in a Westernised, British society that is extremely visual – one which places a lot of emphasis on how we look. You might think that England's capital London and its multicultural society would provide the opportunity and platform for every look, but the media is dominant and still gives more authority and credibility to European features and African-Caribbean people who are the closest to that look.

Many people who have Africentric features want to change them into a more 'acceptable' Eurocentric look. Michael Jackson is a prime example of someone who, in my opinion, has had more facelifts than

I've had hot dinners.

Although he has repeatedly denied cosmetically changing his skin colour, in a rare television interview with Martin Bashir in 2003, Michael disclosed how, as a child, his father ridiculed and often taunted him about his "big" nose.

The cosmetic surgery industry has developed considerably and now reaches global markets as far as Saudi Arabia. Facelifts and nose jobs have become as accessible and affordable as clothes shopping, and I can't see the trend slowing down for sometime – if ever.

As a person now commonly termed 'mixed-race' or 'dual-heritage', my identity has often been the subject of much debate and challenge. This started when I was growing up in the fifties and sixties, when my identity was often under scrutiny by close relatives who tried to define my identity by telling me who I was, and who I wasn't.

For example, my mother would often say, "You're not really black" and compare my skin colour with an object that was visually and obviously black in colour.

"You're missing the point", I would reply, indignant and positive about my blackness, clinging on in the early days to my reality. I knew I wasn't white, but it wasn't just about skin colour either. I knew who and what I was and as challenging as my life experiences have been, this has never changed.

Growing up in an all-white family environment, I had no visual point of reference: I didn't look like anybody in my family. As a young child, I was very dark-skinned with short 'nappy' hair. My complexion became much lighter later on, from my early teens.

It was interesting – but unsurprising – that I then became more 'visually acceptable' to one of my uncles who at first couldn't believe it was me when he saw my photograph. He responded with a 'compliment' about me to my mother saying, "She's turned out to be an attractive girl!"

My mother was always passing on comments made by my distant relatives. I suppose she was trying to make me feel included. However, I saw right through my uncle's prejudices. It would have been far more meaningful to me to be accepted by my uncle when I was a young darker-skinned child rather than later on when I appeared more 'visually acceptable.'

I was the black sheep of the family. I stood out in family photos and felt exposed and far too visible. I wanted so much to blend in and, at times, wanted to disappear. Being an only child, with an absent black father and no siblings to compare myself with, I had to assert my blackness for fear of losing myself.

As a young child I was not in control of my hair. In my mother's opinion, she felt it was better managed short. In those days, there were no trips to hair salons for a trim, and black hairdressers weren't established in the fifties. The hairdressers that did exist wouldn't have been aware of how to treat my mixed-hair. So I often had short misshapen hairdos.

I remember several incidences that relate to my hair. When I was about five or six-years-old, I danced around with a yellow scarf on my head, which I imagined was my long, straight blond hair. This felt good at the time and was as near as I could ever get to feeling like I had long hair. I don't think this has everything to do with being black, but more to do with emulating my mother who had long, wavy ginger hair!

At the age of nine, I remember my mother and me discussing

straightening my hair at the local hairdressers. An appointment was made, but on the day my mother must have sensed my fear and asked me whether I really wanted to go through with it. Thankfully, I declined. Knowing what I know now, it probably would have ruined my hair. It may even have fallen out! Plus, I doubt whether my mother and I would have been able to maintain it without the styling aids, products and hair care awareness we now have.

When I was 11 I got my own way, and my mother stopped cutting my hair. I maintained it by combing it a lot and it grew quite long. I used to put a big slide at the back. I remember my mother saying that I needed to "train" my hair.

I think that white people, more so than black people, perceived me as 'not quite black' and I gained an insight into that perspective. Funny how I never heard, *'You're not really white.'* Only my blackness was an issue and up for discussion.

It was also revealing how some white people would express their racism in different degrees to me by trying to persuade me to ignore my blackness without offering an alternative – they could only tell me that I was visually brown. Sometimes they would say, "You're not like other black people" or "I don't think of you as black." When I wore my hair in an afro, people would say, "If it wasn't for your hair, you wouldn't look black."

This aim by others of trying to deconstruct my identity was challenging. I am so glad that I had American role models like Angela Davis to refer to and support my self-image at that time. The US Black Power movement also gave me and other black people I knew, a sense of pride and a time to celebrate our blackness.

Although some individuals would question my identity, I knew who and what I was. I was committed to my black identity – it was a security against identity confusion and helped me to handle the racism within my family and within wider British society.

My mother, in her own way, tried to encourage me to identify as less than black by choosing 'coloured', whatever that meant at the time. Later, much to my relief and pleasure, and after much dialogue and debate, my mother accepted my identity – my blackness. She saw this as a positive rather than a negative experience. This also gave her the opportunity to challenge racist comments made in my absence. She was able to respond by saying: "Not only do I find that racist remark personally offensive, I am particularly upset by it because my daughter is black."

These challenging experiences forced me to examine my identity and relationships. The difficulty is that as a mixed-race person I was trying to form my identity on my own.

However, despite the challenges from my family and all sorts of ignorant, arrogant and insecure individuals, I managed to define a strong 'sense of self', and develop and value a positive black identity. I saw this as something I wouldn't be without or put another way, I wouldn't be me without it. This kept me safe, positive and strong in a society that measured its people mostly from a white, male and Western perspective.

It isn't problematic that mixed-race people are bi-racial or of dual-heritage; it is that there is so much silence, ignorance and racism.

"We cannot change the colour of our skin. What we can change is how we feel about it. We cannot change a pain-filled past. What we can change is how it affects us. We cannot change how others feel about who we are and where we've been. What we can change is how we see it, how we use it and how others use it to our benefit or detriment. The past has already been written, but we have the power to write the future, based on who we are and what we do now. Only we can write a future based on how much we have grown. We can write a future full of strength, peace, wealth and love. All we have to do is what is right now."

'Acts of Faith Daily Meditations for People of Color', Iyanla Vanzant

BLACK, ACTUALLY

Portia Msimang

"You're a half-caste." Anthony was telling, not asking, me.

"No. I'm not."

At the age of eight, I had never heard that expression before, but I knew that I wasn't one.

"Yes, you are. I've seen your mum and your dad, and you're a half-caste." He stared at me intently; his eyes narrowed behind thick, tinted lenses and his pointed, freckled nose wrinkled.

I had never liked Anthony. His shrill, lisping voice interrupted every lesson to ask stupid questions that had really simple answers or no real answers. He laughed at anything and he cried over nothing. He began to laugh and point at me.

"And before you came to this school, you were running around naked in Africa."

Now, he had given me a reason to hate him.

"No I wasn't!" He had embarrassed me.

"Yes you were. You told me before, ages ago, when I was looking at a book. I was reading and you came to tell me that. Don't you remember? I remember."

"I didn't say that." He was really hurting me, somewhere soft, deep down between my bony ribs, and that pain made my ears ache. I felt like crying, but I knew that if I did people would gather round and ask me what was wrong and I would have to repeat the embarrassing, horrible things that Anthony had said to me, starting with "half-caste".

"Really, you're mixed-race," Rachel told me, 30 years on.

"Ouch!" I replied, with as much coldness as can be imparted into a single syllable. I was surprised, but I had grown used to hearing it. I had grown hard where once I was soft.

"Does that offend you?"

"Yes."

"It really shouldn't. Hey, it's no big deal. I mean, I guess I'm mixed-race myself. I'm a mix of Nigerian and Jamaican and who knows what else," she drawled.

Because I like Rachel, because we were talking on her telephone bill, because it was very late in the day and I was too tired to argue, I moved the conversation on instead. I asked how her studies were coming along and she admitted how tired she was of working by day and studying accountancy at night.

"It'll soon be over and you're going to have a major sense of achievement." That's what friends are for.

Last Christmas, I went shopping for presents in a bookshop in Piccadilly, London, with an elderly friend. His initials are WW and he derived great satisfaction from the free gift-wrapping service. "Perfectly monogrammed," he chuckled, tapping the top of his pile of books, all covered in white paper, printed in black with uppercase Ws in various fonts.

An hour later, when we were about to part at Cannon Street train station, he realised that he had left his purchases behind, in the bookshop's café, where we had celebrated a most successful afternoon's shopping with a pot of Earl Grey. I offered to go back for the books. He agreed.

By the time I rushed back, the store had grown as quiet as a library. There was the space to notice the tall, pale walls surrounding vibrant book displays and shelves showing bound spines of every shade and hue. At the 'Enquiries' desk, I was told that the forgotten books were now in the security office. In contrast to the airy, elegant glow of the shop floor, the security office was small, stuffy and dimly lit. I noticed that every member of uniformed security staff was black.

Weighed down with WW's pile of hardbacks I left, walking more slowly than when I had arrived. I had time to look around. I observed that, with the exception of one South Asian woman, every member of the sales staff on the ground floor was white. I wondered whether I was witnessing the globalisation of apartheid.

The architects of apartheid promoted their dirty propaganda of 'equal but separate' and classified people not just into 'black' and 'white', but also Chinese and Indian as 'coloured'.

The appalling inequity, injustice and brutality of the apartheid era in Southern Africa (for variants existed in the countries now called Namibia and Zimbabwe, as well as in The Republic of South Africa) are indisputable. Those crude but elaborate systems of privilege and control amply demonstrated that there can be no society where people are both separate and equal.

Lizzie is white. Her daughter is black. "I like her to think of herself as mixed-race," Lizzie told me from the driver's seat as we sped down the motorway one afternoon, "to reflect both sides of her heritage."

Like both her parents, the little girl was born, and had always lived, in London.

"She's black, though." I tried not to grit my teeth.

"Well, I'm her mum and I'm white, so she's not all black."

"My mum's white and I'm black."

"Yes, but you are black of mixed-parentage so you are mixed-race." She spoke in that bright, patient tone most often reserved for a tiresomely quizzical child.

Science has proved that the concept of race has no biological basis. The differences between people are slight; variations in physical characteristics have evolved to enable our survival across different geographical regions.

Skin colour is little more than a balancing act between the evolutionary demands of photo-protection and vitamin production. Even the word 'race' sounds increasingly archaic, inextricably linked to European colonial adventures and to Nazism.

Race is a social, cultural and political concept based upon

superficial appearances and the weight of history. Why would anyone encourage her child to think of herself in terms of 'race'? Does Lizzie fear that being black would harm her child's prosperity, and the opportunity to achieve her full human potential?

In a global context, monetary wealth is concentrated in countries with a predominantly white population. Wherever we are born in the world, though, the chances of growing up poor are greater for those of us whose skin colour is other than white. According to the Office for National Statistics 2001/02, over 20% of black men are unemployed in Britain compared with 12% of white British men.

Although youth unemployment is generally higher than the national average, this unhappy statistic reflects more than the comparative youth of the Black British population as a whole. I wonder whether Lizzie knows that, in Britain, the unemployed who identify as being mixed-race are very similar to the black population as a whole.

"In Trinidad, we all know the name of the game. If you're white, you're alright, if you're brown, come on down and if you're black, stand back," Dana laughed. I heard bitter pain, anger and frustration in that laugh. I smiled in acknowledgement, but I did not laugh. The division that leads to discrimination is no laughing matter.

"It is exactly that mentality which built apartheid." My Father spat out the words, not at me, but I heard him, anyway. "There is nothing wrong with being either black or white. There is nothing inherently good or bad in either but what, exactly, do you think you mean by mixed-race?"

His South African accent is never more pronounced than when he is angry, and his accent was very much in evidence that day. He has lived through this struggle before and he is always ready for war. He knows how apartheid was constructed because he was there.

Here and now, we are in a position to abandon the scientifically discredited, morally repugnant philosophies, which have elsewhere demonstrably decreased the vulnerability of those who are willing to embrace their status as 'mulatto', 'coloured', or 'mixed-race'. This has always served to the detriment of all black people. It is false sophistry to argue that any of these terms is less offensive than another.

There is no 'separate but equal'. When I look in the mirror, a black woman reflects back at me. In those eyes, there is a slight weariness from 30 years of arguing to be allowed to be black. Most people will never get close enough to notice. The reflection I see in windows, at approximately the distance of the world, walks with head held high because inside it, I carry my heritage, the unshakeable belief in world citizenship, with great care.

HOT BREAD

Desiree Senior

My father rises from his seat and slowly makes his way to the television, not once taking his eyes from it. I believe that he thinks his intense concentration will turn up the volume on the set until he gets his hands on the remote control, which is sitting on top of the TV set.

He is sitting back down now. You would never know that we had just engaged in a warm exchange of historical experience and knowledge.

My mother sits opposite me, writing in total concentration and breathing heavily. To my right, on the floor, is the most beautiful of my few possessions in my still very unorthodox life – my daughter, Sankofa Bird. With a past so wonderful, her future is sure to be an adventurous flight.

As I look around me, I feel nothing has changed. My sister does not sit with us on this spring evening, but her very person seems to sit within Sankofa Bird: assertive, cheeky and so funny. She is my sister all over again.

As I reflect on my childhood, like the days that my Sankofa Bird now experiences, my memories are vivid. I recall many other similar evenings, in this very front room: the smell of that time; the feelings I harbour within my four-year-old self.

My mother worked constantly. My father never awoke later than 4.30am. My sister and I were similar in age, yet vastly different in personality, very like my parents. My mother stood for all that was contrived and well spoken. She was small framed and always smelled of the hospital.

She was also our nurse, a disciplinarian, and she was unmistakably black. Her features were those of our native African women. You know the ones you see on batiks with a child in arms. She was, to me, Royalty. She moved gracefully and whispered when she spoke, and spoke when she shouted.

My father was white, or so everybody thought, with fair skin and blue eyes. He was so 'sweet'. It came to be a word I would hear from friends for years to come and one that would become meaningless.

"Your dad, ah, he's so..."

"...sweet?" I would finish their sentence.

"Yeah.. sweet, that's what I was gonna say."

Dad was softly spoken. He was a thinker, a deep thinker. I guess that is why he never said much. Either that or there wasn't much wrong with anything. However, I knew then as has been confirmed now, that my father was a dreamer. This highly intelligent man had not yet made it back to his homeland, Jamaica, to touch down with those from the village. He wished to travel by boat. He still wishes.

My childhood memories begin some 24 years ago when I was in an internal battle to realise who I was and how I fitted into my family mosaic. School was the best place to be, but some days it could be strange and challenging. Today I would have friends, tomorrow I would have none, and as this raw exchange of emotion would take place, so too would the search for the answer to the questions about my identity.

Looking back, the schoolyard banter was a catalyst that encouraged me to look at myself the way others saw me. I always saw myself as the sister of the daughter of...but school had given me a new title – half-caste. And with this title came two questions: 'Are you black?' and 'Is your dad white?' To which my answer was always, "I don't know."

On my right knee I bore all the proof that was needed to affiliate me with white parentage, a strawberry birthmark. On such a tiny person, the mark was huge! It was neither pink nor a lighter shade of brown but white. There was no way, when participating in typical school activities, that this mark could be disguised.

It became apparent that those who would continuously ask me these questions were children who looked like me, and in the same tone that they would ask the question, they would humiliate and demoralise me no matter what response I gave them.

My school days seemed to blend into one, long unforgiving series of questions: Who? Where? When? Why? I remember walking home with my mother in silence knowing that all the kids in the schoolyard were taking in how different my mother and I were, planning to make it an issue in tomorrow's banter. I felt as if I was walking 'The Famished Road' in a constant search to find peace in my environment, and inner peace to the questions that seemed too complex to be bothering my frame at such a young age.

My skin colour, I had noticed, was no more different than most of the black children in the school, but I was the lightest of us all. My hair appeared to be of the same texture as the others. I spoke the same language as I understood their tongue. So what was it about me that made me so disliked among my own people? Why did it feel like a power I couldn't fight? And why did it hurt so much?

The Blues Brothers sang, 'Everybody, needs somebody', and I guess this little somebody needed for everybody to like her 'cause maybe – just maybe – she didn't.

What could she do to be more liked? There appeared to be only two options: be more like the darker children or be more like the lighter children. There were allies in either camp although, on reflection, it was not apparent that the lighter skinned children had a problem – they liked me.

My best friend was white and she and I would spend many a day singing and playing in the schoolyard between being beaten up by a black girl and her gang. I say we but – if the truth were known – it was me the gang had the problem with. As for my best friend, well she just did the best friend thing – she shared the beatings.

Throughout my time at primary school, I never begged an adult for an answer to why these things were happening to me. I knew that these things were not happening to my sister. My sister was darker than me and had no trouble making friends. She was a build that made other children think twice before messing with her, and so her schoolyard fate was already foretold.

Yet outside of school, I was having the best time ever. My best friend and I spent wonderful days together and, on reflection, we were doing nothing more than tasting and experiencing each other's culture.

Methodist church, then a full roast dinner. Catholic church followed by rice and peas, stew chicken and the tastiest, softest hot bread. My friend would continuously ask where these foods, especially the hot bread, came from. My mother would always promise to take us there 'one day'. Within this friendship, I found security within myself and in the world. This person was different from me, but she never saw my colour, or did she?

The summer holidays had come to an abrupt end. The day steadily approached for me to return to school. My summer holidays had been great, yet again. My best friend and I had spent endless hours together. I had taken up a hobby – gymnastics.

I returned to school dreading the comments that not only would come from those who already knew me, but those who were new to me. It was to be a whole new induction during PE with *that* birthmark on my knee. Shorts and a t-shirt; legs exposed equals:

"Urgh!"

"What is that?"

"Are you white then?"

We sat eagerly, waiting to hear what the term's new activity was to be. My guess was something that always seemed to last forever, something I really couldn't relate to, like barn dancing! However, to my surprise, it was gymnastics.

We were all put into groups to do different activities. The question was did I do these activities to the best of my ability, which was easy, or should I to do them badly so that I wouldn't stand out anymore than I did already? I chose the latter and proceeded to complete the tasks badly, or so I thought.

The class was called to a halt after 10 minutes of 'having a go'. Then we were asked to sit down quietly. The teacher beckoned me with her finger. I turned to look behind me before facing her. She beckoned and again I looked behind me until I realised it was me she wanted.

As I walked to the front of the class, my face felt as if it was going to fry. Looking back, I wonder, what colour was I at that precise moment? I know I had been fooling about, trying hard to do my worst, as someone who had grave difficulty in attempting a cartwheel or forward roll.

Instead, the teacher whispered in my ear, "I can see that you are very good. Can you show them how to do it properly?" And with that, an announcement was made to the class that I was going to demonstrate a cartwheel. Off I went cartwheeling across the gym, non-stop, to the 'gasps' and 'wows' of my peers. When I finished, it was to a round of applause. There were no comments about my colour or my parents as cartwheeling did not require knowledge of your lineage.

As time passed, I became known as the girl who could back flip, do the splits and cartwheel. Many times I was asked to represent the school and teach my newfound skills to my peers. But I couldn't or wouldn't pass on the one thing that gave me peace, the one thing that had led to the transference of attention from my outstanding appearance to my outstanding achievement; one that everyone could share in.

One afternoon, I decided to ask my father the question that had plagued me prior to my newfound fame. I no longer felt alienated at school, quite the opposite, but I often wondered if I didn't have this talent, where would I stand?

My father was waiting for me to come home. My sister was riding her tricycle outside. As I looked at her, I couldn't help but think that she was the same colour as those who taunted me at school. Was she also going to do the same thing to me? In fact, were all people of that shade going to do the same thing to me?

I sat down at my dad's feet and waited for him to ask me how my day at school was. When he did, my response was, "Dad, are you white?" At that moment, it seemed as if the world had slowed down as an array of emotions crossed his face: pity, sadness, empathy and then anger. I had definitely said the wrong thing, and I was convinced that this was the end of my short-lived evening.

But no sooner had I convinced myself that now was as good a time as any to vacate the room, my father sat me on his knee. He explained why God had made us so different, and why some people would think he was white when, in fact, he was a black man born of a white man and a black woman.

The colour of his skin, I understood, was a representation of where and who he had come from; those who had passed through his blood line before he was born was manifest in all of us. He believed that he was a black man, reminding me of the texture of his hair and the ambiguous shape of his nose. To this day, I have never asked him why he has never considered himself mixed-race, as he clearly is.

The morning after our conversation, I couldn't help but feel that my talk with daddy had created an awkwardness in the family household. Maybe I had questioned areas of my father's life that he never questioned before. Or had I opened closed wounds?

Saturday morning had arrived. It was the day for the weekly shop. Mum would leave the house the same time each Saturday and return with goodies galore. But today was to be different. Today, we were to go as a family. We arrived at the superstore and followed mum and dad to the various aisles that revealed where all our tasty morsels came from, where all the sweet smelling liquids were purchased and finally...where the hot bread we ate every Saturday morning was made.

There it was – the in store bakery with all manner of breads in different shapes, sizes, colours and textures, freshly made, waiting for hungry shoppers to pluck them from the shelves and transport them home for the post shopping brekkie. We chose our loaf carefully, making sure we had the biggest and hottest one in the store. We carried it tenderly back to the car.

The whole loaf never made it home. This became our ritual: sisters on the back seat eating that fresh hot loaf from the inside out. All that was left when we arrived home was half a loaf with a hollow shell.

How tasty that bread was, and how selective my sister and I were in trying a different loaf every week. How good they all tasted, the different textures a gastronomic adventure. It didn't matter to us if the bread had seeds or not, if it were white or brown, as long as it was hot and tasted good. We were satisfied every Saturday morning.

The weekly experience of choosing hot bread was to remain with me into adulthood. For among such a vast selection of bread that all looked, felt and tasted so different, they all had the same potential: to make wicked sandwiches!

Interviews

BISI AKINOLA

"I identify with black people, but I also identify with white people because I was fostered by a white family.

I was privately fostered in Birmingham, from six weeks to four-years-old. It was a Nigerian thing to do. My dad was studying and my mum was working in Derby. Luckily for me, three out of the four children of the lady who fostered us went out with black people. They had black friends. Black music was always on. They listened to old reggae and lovers rock. When I was at home with my parents, I heard Nigerian music. I went back and forth between my parents and foster home every couple of weeks.

When I was writing for the anthology my foster mum was ill. She had cancer. I was there when she died, so she was basically my mum. At my foster mum's wake, there was curry goat and rice.

You would think that with the white connection there would be no blackness in my life. But I had my family and her family. So I didn't lose my identity. Maybe my foster experience enhanced it.

At 23 I had my first poem *Is Anyone There?* published on www.poetry.com. It was to do with the famine in Sudan. I paid to have it published. Afterwards I thought, I'm not going to pay for my work to be published any more.

Writing my submission *QUEEN*, felt good. I host QUEEN nights where my black friends come round and we natter. I feel like a queen. It is part of my identity.

I don't want my poems just to be classed as black writing, though I don't write in old style English like Shakespeare. I write poetry so people understand it.

I'm a teacher. I have to be flexible with everybody in my job. When I first started teaching in state schools for European foreign language students I was the only black teacher. It didn't bother me because I was there on my own merits.

But black and white people would ask, what colour is your boyfriend? I found that quite offensive. What relevance is it? My husband is black. They think my partner is white because I can relate to white people.

They treat my name like it's a nickname. If a black person laughs at my name, I think why are you laughing? Aren't we all African?

Singers inspire me more than writers. Mary J Blige does that for me. When she sings, it's poetry. I go to poetry jams. Everything there is personal, but because someone is saying it you can interpret it, which makes me want to keep my own style."

TABITHA CUMMINS

"Making a submission to this anthology was such a hard process. The essay I wrote – *What Colour is Black?* – touched too close to home. I thought the piece would be misunderstood. To be honest, I really wanted to run away from it, but I felt it was important to express the other side of the story.

Although UK culture is set up for people to make an instant judgement on a person's colour, I feel it happens when you first open your mouth. Those first few seconds when you speak, combined with how you dress, are what counts.

Judgements like, *this girl is trying to be white* or *that girl is trying to be black*. That's partly why I was scared of sending in my work.

The first thing I wrote was a song. I was 15. I had something of a burn inside me and it had to come out, and it did, in poetic form. I've had stuff published in church journals and magazines. I did a play two years ago, which was performed at Regent's Hall on Oxford Street in London. But that's it.

My parents are from Barbados. I don't necessarily look black. I have very dark hair. So anything with dark hair and olive skin I get mistaken for: Mediterranean, Latin American, Asian.

I have two younger sisters. We are all different shades. Yet we are always asked, are you from different parents? My youngest sister is darker than me. When she gets up, she is instantly judged as a black woman. When I get up I face sly digs.

Unless I open my mouth, you wouldn't realise that I am black. But we are supportive of each other as sisters in the face of people's dismissal and disapproval.

With all the challenges, it is important to remain feminine and not forget that you are a woman. There is a tendency to hide your emotional side, which is something I do. To cope with work pressures, women put on this whole tough front.

It is important for women, especially black women, to have an outlet for the other sides of their personalities, to be more creative, sensual, loving, and caring.

When I was 16, I went through this black power phase. Everything I read was black or had black overtones. Then I realised that God created me this way and for a reason. I bring a lot to the black race, but I also open up the eyes of white people.

I've sat with white women who say something [about race] and don't realise who I am. I let them know that what they are saying is about me. It's easier for them to take it from me. It isn't necessarily a good thing, but it gets the message across.

Maya Angelou and Toni Morrison have been my biggest writing influences. Jane Austin also inspires me. But the bible has had a huge influence on my style of writing. I would like my writing to have that same type of universal appeal."

DANIELLE IMBERT

"I'd written the poem *All Mixed Up* for a documentary I did at university. It was about mixed-race identity.

The reason I did the documentary was because of the myth about mixed-race people being confused. My starting point was, with so many people and so many books and editorials on mixed-race people's confusion, it must be true.

When I first started interviewing people for my documentary, I tried to persuade them to tell me about their troubled childhood. But they kept saying it wasn't troubled. So I thought maybe they were lying, and wondered: why weren't they telling me the truth? By the end I thought this isn't necessarily true, not nowadays. In the past, maybe.

My mum is white English and my dad is from Mauritius. I've been mistaken for every racial identity: Turkish, Mexican, half-caste, mixed-race! It's just annoying and has been since I was about 13. In the winter I go really pale, in the summer I get a tan and I go as dark as many light-skinned black people.

I went to Tunisia last year. When I was walking through the hotel this man spoke to me in Arabic. I said, 'I'm English'. He replied, 'but you are from here'. I repeated, 'I'm English'. He asked me where my parents were from. I tried to explain my heritage. By the end of my holiday the hotel staff were calling me '50/50'.

I don't know if being mixed-race is better or worse in the UK than anywhere else. Maybe it is worse in America, where they think if you are not white, you are black.

Sometimes, when I am with a group of white friends, I'm more self-conscious. Once, while getting ready to go out, everyone decided to wear jeans. I wanted to wear a skirt, but I didn't want to stand out and look different from everyone else. I also didn't want us to all look the same. It didn't seem to be about race at the time, but when you sit down and think about it…. Maybe I am trying to individualise myself a bit more without really thinking about it. That's why I love writing poetry. I entered a poetry competition when I was about 16. Both poems got through to the semi-finals and were published in two books. I haven't seen copies of the books.

It doesn't feel like there are any books out there by mixed-race people. Everything I have ever read is from a black perspective or a white perspective; writers who think they know what mixed-race people are thinking.

I don't think that a black female writer is in a position to comment on being mixed-raced. You can learn from each other, but don't write about something you don't have personal experience of.

I hope my work and the '*Brown Eyes*' anthology gives people a sense of what mixed-race people go through. I hope they understand that you are not white and you are not black. That there is something different and that's okay."

BIANCA VICTORIA JOSEPH

"Trying to find out who you are is obviously hard when you have two people from different races as parents. But once you get there it is good because you find yourself and you can concentrate on the advantages rather than the disadvantages of it. As I grow up (I'm only 13-years-old), the disadvantages won't bother me as much.

It sounds silly, but I can't kiss my teeth. I just can't do it. My friends say it's because you are mixed-race. I just laugh and say it has nothing to do with being mixed-race, it's because I just can't do it.

I've been writing since I was seven. The first poem I wrote was about being told to go to bed by my mum. I'm a writer not just a poet. I really enjoy English. I've had work published through school.

Every year, we are given a different subject to write about. The best poems are selected and published in a young writers' book, covering schools from different areas. I've had my work published three years in a row. Being chosen is inspiring. It just makes me want to write better poems.

I thought my poem *MIXED* would be good for this anthology because it is about mixed-race people and how it is a struggle, but how it is also a good thing to have white and black in you. I'm not trying to hammer it into your head that it's either good or hard to be mixed-race. It's for people to make up their own mind. I try to be balanced.

There are good things about being mixed-race. You can identify with both your black and white sides. You also have the two different points of view. With me my mum is Italian and my dad is Dominican. On the Italian side, I really love the culture. It is really friendly. On the Dominican side, I love the food and the country is beautiful. I'm closer to my dad's family than my mum's because they live in Italy.

I'm light-skinned with mainly Afro-Caribbean hair, so people do get confused about where I'm from. Sometimes strangers will have little discussions between themselves before they come over and talk to you. It is funny to watch and see the confusion while they try and figure it out.

One of the advantages of living in London is that there are more mixed-race people. But one of the disadvantages is that when you see other mixed-race people you ask the same questions that you don't like being asked about yourself. Things like, 'I wonder where she is from?' Or 'she has really nice hair. I wonder where her parents are from?' That's why I don't get so annoyed when people do that to me. I like books about my age group that I can identify with rather than fantasy books. *Sorelle* is a good book. It's about a black girl who thinks that she will never ever like an Asian person and she ends up falling in love with an Asian boy. Books like that are interesting, but there aren't that many of them around."

BEIGE

When will our skin colour
be just a colour?

Poems

I am BeautifulLovingAttractiveCaringKind

Being a darker shade of brown is okay
Stand up straight, say it loud
I am a beautiful black woman and I am proud

Trials and tribulations will come your way
But being the woman you are
You will make it through the day

Whether you are a darker or lighter shade of black
Don't let others' harsh words hold you back
Life is for living so live it your best
Deep down inside do you want to be like the rest?

Know who you are
And know who you ain't
Just because you are black
Don't mean you can't be a saint

Be proud of who you are
Because I know that I am
I'm going to keep on doing
The best that I can

Stereotypes and lies made to discriminate
So what have you done that makes people hate
You just because of the colour of your skin
You've committed no crime, committed no sin

Hold your head up high, my sister,
Yes, I'm talking to you
We should be sticking together
Because there's a lot we've been through

Bisi Akinola

Sour Grapes

Which do you prefer
white or black grapes?
I don't really care
It's the bitter pips that I really hate

I hear them arguing all the time
always about silly things
What exactly do they say?
This and that mainly about who they think is king

My black grapes are sweeter than yours
my black grapes are bigger than yours
my black grapes are more expensive than yours
my black grapes are better than yours

Who says so?

Well, my white grapes might not be as sweet but they are fresh
my white grapes might be smaller but they don't all have pips
my white grapes might be cheaper but they are not less worthy
and no black grapes are better than me

Who says so?

Well, our seed may produce different coloured grapes
but we are still grapes
we are both going to be washed, eaten
spat out and forgotten

So you are saying that we have to live together
despite our skin colour
and to forget about sour grapes
in order to make our life fuller?

That's exactly what I am saying my 'brother'
because us grapes don't have any other
it seems to be me to be so absurd
that we can't live together in this tiny, tiny, world

I ain't better than you
and you aren't better than me
the sooner our grapes understand that fact
the sweeter our pips will be

Bisi Akinola

How Long

How long will we continue to judge a person by their race & skin
   colour?
Their sex & sexuality, their physical features & disabilities,
Their accent, class & financial status?

How long will we continue to starve one another of food, love & life?

How long will we continue to allow the exploitation of our people?

How long will we continue to cheat one another & ourselves?

How long will we continue to shoot & stab one another over
   pettiness?

How long will we continue to chat & curse one another?

How long will we continue to destroy each other?

How long will we continue to watch our children having children?

How long will we continue to watch the raping of our women?

How long will we continue to watch the emasculation of our men?

How long will we continue to suffer in silence?

How long will we continue to be content with our condition?

How long will we continue to allow the system to beat us?

How long will we continue to be passive victims of circumstance?

How long will we continue to sink in the blood of oppression?

How long will our ancestors continue to toss & turn in their graves with dismay & disgust?

When will we become active participants?
When will we free ourselves from bondage?
When will we stop stalling & answer gods calling?
When will we come together in our plight?
When will we all stand & unite?
When…..when…..when?

Tonya Joy Bolton

Black

Black
A colour so whole
A colour with soul
Real soul, you know
I speak not the soul of mind
But the soul of heart
You clearly tell us apart
From those who contrast
You know who in which I talk
We are the soul of Arts
Literature, science, crafts
And many more, which we led the path

Black
A colour so powerful
A colour so humble
Yes noble, and fruitful
My eyes see it as pure
Yet, the dictionary dictates it as raw
Foul, evil and unclean
Why Babylon have to be so mean
Destroy fiercely the elements that are unseen
Like the mind that is captured and lost
So many generations paid the cost
And still, we maintain so much love
And hate that generates from the oppression we suffer
Jah don't stop bless us, like no other

Black
As pure as the eyes can see
As deep as the ocean or the sea
It's the rudiments before there was life
As there was darkness before there was light
It's the bottomless hole
It's the fire with the coal
It's Black...rich Black...passionate Black
Black

Monique Campbell

We

We, came from a family of strong women.
Women who could separate mountains from the seas with one hand
and cook a feast for a king with the other.
Their strength had carried generations
and in their care thousands came to be born.
Their fingers had moulded the heads of kings
and shaped the spines of queens.
Their feet had travelled a million miles to new worlds
braving distant seas.
With their lips they built dreams
and with their thoughts carved out new destinies.
So naturally it came as a surprise to me
when my four brothers as a group and individually
told me that their brides to be
would never resemble "We".
You see,
the strength "We" had running through our veins
in this Western world was not an attractive quality.
"I mean, I haven't got anything against black girls," they said
"but black girls just aren't for me."
You see,
"We" would never truly fit the pages of GQ, Loaded or Vanity,
so what else to do but cash your chips in and try for better things.
"A professional black man must always be seen with the right
accessories and I'm trying to make it in this white-man's world and
colour just ain't a thing".

Tolu Melissa Carew

Grievance

A grievance, from a brown skin born;

Resting on the disarray of popular confusion
My beautiful skin
Is unable to complete the promise of its magnificence

For the troops that power our cultural rights
A disorientated tag is placed on the mixed-races
For we lack a 'fit': categorised as 'our own', yet not

My forefathers brought me together
Each, bearing a gifted gene
From every corner of this earth
In the beauty of every colour

Blind, have been the purveyors of my fate
And docile have been those
With the power to break this curse
Bearing yet another promise, a new name

Tagged against political correctness
The struggle is already led
Onto the battlefield of betterment
And I court my strength to present
A request, from a brown skin born;

Know me; this is all I can be.

Nicola Greenwood

Label or Instruction?

I am wearing 100% cotton mix judgement

Some labels say:

Wash at 30 degrees
Do not mix with dark colours
Line Dry; Iron Medium

My favourite labels say:

Open eyes at 360 degrees
Mix all the colours
Try love; Iron racism

Made on Earth – every colour available.

Nicola Greenwood

BEIGE: When will our skin colour be just a colour?

Progression

They're blocking me from *progression,* trying to cause my regression
They can't abide, that I preside
Adept and articulate, thinking *how ridiculous*
She's a woman, sole parent and black!
We can't let her progress, *not someone like that!*

I don't fit into their *Oxbridge* ideal, I come from the streets *I'm real*
I grew up in south London, *Peckham*, raised by my Caribbean mum
I rate myself second to none and I can't be made to run
Not afraid to speak my mind, about discrimination I find
I know my rights and represent all those people that *they* resent

They call me an ethnic minority but not with my consent
I define myself as a majority and that term they use I resent
Only have to look at the world to see we make up the majority
That term they use is mental slavery, designed to undermine you
  and me

So they're blocking my progression call it a permanent recession
Don't want to see someone of *my* gender and race
Honour their executive boards with my grace
But when I tell them how I feel, give it to them straight, *remember
  I'm real*
They tell me they find me aggressive, confrontational and excessive

But you know if I was white and male, educated at Oxford,
Cambridge or even Yale
They'd tell me I was assertive, sensational and progressive
But remember I'm an ethnic *majority*, my ancestors fought *slavery*
And like a suffragette, it's not over yet

Because I'll rise above them one day soon, despite their secret chants of nigger and coon

You see I'm fired with a flame that will burn out all their shame
I may not rise to fame, but I can play them at their own game
And though they won't give me a level playing field
To disseminate all I yield

Just remember I've combatted *sexism, racism, fascism and oppression*
Simultaneously, not in *succession*
And I'm still standing, still achieving and there's no way I am leaving
They may block my progression in the workplace, but I will always achieve, see this face!

They may shut doors in it, spit at it, look down on it, disregard it
But still I shine in the face of adversity and I didn't need to go to
   university
To figure out what they're about
I may be a woman and I may be black, but know something – I'm
   proud of that

Life isn't a concession, and I've got a confession
I overcame multiple oppression, so I sure as hell don't need
   permission
To achieve promotion or progression and that's the end of this
   lesson

Zita Holbourne

All I Can Want is What There Is

Futuristic slave ship, ex-polytechnic
Where is this?
Will it last? Contrived?
Camera eyes are canteen wise
As if coffee, chocolate, tea – are the common sense
And all art is of abstract importance.
To reward rations of race
With style and substance
The vocational violence of freedom
Going around my rebellion
As European rivers of national treasures
Swamp frozen, time and thought
In their old search for older men?
I begin to mix skin with conscience
As I bid for independence
All I can want is what there is.

The urban carousel of hard stares
European, African and Asian ears!
To have the last word:
Remarks made of shrapnel
They sound so personal
Are they tribal or virtual?
All colours treat lives like shades
Like safe bait
Tight in their skin, possessive in pace
All features fester
And colour my self-defence
That skin is the screen of the voice
Like I don't have choice

The channel trying to escape, but
Submerged for money of my own.

Emma Louise Felicia Hopkins

Mixed

What is black?
Or what is white,
What is a person who is both?
Dark and light

Why be black
Or why be white,
When you're a person in
Your own right,

When can silver be mixed with gold,
When will people realise the untold?

So I ask you one more time

What is black?
Or what is white,
Mixed is the person who is
Both dark and light.

Bianca Victoria Joseph

An Acquired Pastime

African Woman your rhythm captivates me
Unhurried elegant and majestically graceful
Pulsating first wonder of the world
You whose beauty is not accepted,
popularised celebrated nor paraded
on covers and centrefolds.
African Woman you are Africa's gold minds;
the unsung treasure of her wealth and riches.
The effortless sway of your robust hips
cradles the spirit of your balance.

African Woman rhythm clouds adorn your skies.
Even in your shuffle ancient sambas
are encapsulated in your slow motion.
The mystery in your eyes translate your longing.
Your smile radiates the power of your heart.
Black-gem, pearl of black, mother-earth;
you who cannot be invisible-eyed.
I see you in your splendour perhaps for the first time
now that I see in my extended awareness of beauty
African! Beauty!

Jackie Lewis

I Live in a Matt Neighbourhood

In my neighbourhood
Colours have not experienced free flow,
So they linger in half-truths
And hover in mellow magnificence.
Colours slumbering
In faded pastel saturation.
Blues are not true to form
Yellows weep like willows
Greens arch and billow.
In absence of their serenity
Splendour is never in full bloom
And flame hot oranges
Are dull and matt,
Their vibrancy consumed.

Jackie Lewis

What Makes her Name

Just a woman like any other,
Feminine with curves and a delicate touch.
Just a woman like any other,
Softly spoken but words mean much.

Just a woman like any other,
The fertility cycle leads to a brand new start.
Just a woman like any other,
From Mars she will always stand apart.

Just a woman like any other,
She stares at the mirror to inspect herself.
Just a woman like any other,
Often her beauty is her wealth.

But some see her reflection with poor sight
Some see dark where there is light
Some mistake her weight for her might
Mistake her fist for her fight
But her cause is just.

Not just the physical but the mental struggle
The many problems that she must juggle
But she is not just trouble and strife.
She is mother. She is sister. She is wife

Not just a woman like any other.
With her X factor she marks the spot.
Not just a woman like any other.
She constantly drops it like it's hot.

In the kitchen soul food is cooking.
Her food for thought will keep you looking.

See the afro, ain't all that she be.
There's more than skin to her diversity.
And sure she's subject to the questions you ask
About the depth, state and the effect of her mask
If that's what you perceive her essence to be.

"But it's not attire belonging to she"
Like her broken dialect –
It's the clouded visions you collect
As you try to entrap her.

She may be alone but she is spiritual.
Remembering from where she came.
Remembering what makes her name.
Remembering who she is.

Fiona Mckinson

Brown Eyes

Glad to be Me...

As I played in the playground
I'd often be called something "black".
Teased and tormented,
Told to go back!

Yet when I fell over
And they saw that my blood was red.
It was hard for them
To get it in their head!

"She's bleeding red blood!
Look... it's not black!"
They crowded so much the teacher had to come
And hold them back!

I think they realised then
That I came from this earth
I was human
Not a piece of dirt.

I had been made as God wanted me.
This is my colour, and I am free.
We have no choice once we are born.
The colour from our skin cannot be torn.

So to all the children in the playground, who ask,
This is my blessing, my pride is not a mask!
I have a culture, so rich and so vast
Why not look up some of these great people
Set that as your task!

Nelissa Mendy

Colour

Colour, hue, I just love you
And your colour
Brown tones
Honey sweet shades
Of a deep and strongness

Skin deep, soft and mellow
A lighter degree of shade
Like the Sun reflecting
Powerful – a shining star
Amongst the twilight zone

But it's more than just a colour
That creates fear amongst ignorance
It's the unknown face
Of difference

Nicole Moore

Essays

NOTES OF A BLACK WOMAN

Deborah Akinpelu

I went to visit an old friend of mine the other day. I hadn't seen her in a while. It was a beautiful sunny day, and I was happy to be back home after what seemed like a very long time. You see I only get to see my parents once a year – twice if I'm lucky.

On the way to my friend's, I was confronted with something I hadn't dealt with for a while – the staring. I wasn't used to being stared at anymore, although a few years ago it was part of my daily routine. It was 'normal' to be stared at when you were black. It was so blatant that even if you said something offensive to the person, the staring wouldn't stop.

My name is Dee. I'm originally from Nigeria, but was born and raised in Vienna, Austria. Austria isn't as multicultural as London. That said, I notice that my being an 'Afro-Austrian' in London draws quite a lot of curiosity and attention.

People find it interesting because they don't expect blacks to live in countries other than Africa, the UK, North and South America, the Caribbean Islands, for instance. Yet, I am sure that you would find at least two handfuls of blacks in China.

Before I proceed, I would like you to understand that right from kindergarten to secondary school, I have always been the only black child, so I would like you to judge what I write rather carefully.

"What is your name, dear?" the elderly lady asked the little girl sitting beside her on the bus.

"My name is Dee,' the girl replied.

"You speak good German. Where are you from?" the lady exclaimed.

"I'm from Vienna."

The elderly lady smiled, looking puzzled.

Bedtime. Dee gets down on her knees to say her nightly prayer:

"Dear Lord, when I wake up tomorrow, would you let me be a white girl with long blond hair and blue eyes? Amen."

Of course she never woke up blond-haired and blue-eyed. Growing up, she accepted the fact that she could never look like 'the others', yet she definitely was like 'the others'. At the age of 10, she was confronted with minor racial problems at school, but they didn't discourage her from wanting to be 'white'.

She would clip her nose together with a peg to attain a pointed nose. She wouldn't remove it until either the pain became unbearable or she was in danger of acute suffocation.

On other occasions she would press her lips together (she had quite full lips as opposed to her younger sister) to make them look 'thinner'. She would even stare at her palms for a very long time, wondering why the rest of her body couldn't look like that.

Not that she particularly disliked her skin colour, but it is the mid-eighties when many Austrians still believed that blacks were dark because they either didn't wash themselves or they had been burnt to charcoal by a very angry sun. Quite often Dee was asked if she washed herself and scrubbed herself "really, really hard", would she turn white. She said, yes.

It was also the mid-eighties when quite a few Austrians still believed that Africans and monkeys all lived in the same house (aka trees), and dined together. This belief held on tightly into the early nineties. In her teens, Dee was asked whether Africa had heard about television, cable or satellite TV.

When she turned 13, her aunt introduced her to the relaxer, a chemical hair-straightening system. Dee felt part of her dreams were coming true. Soon she would have long straight hair. It would finally be the end of the long, dreaded Sundays spent sitting by the gas stove, body trembling, waiting for her mother to straighten (or singe) her hair with a steaming hot straightening comb that sparked each time it ran through her hair. She feared that her head might catch on fire.

It would be the end of shying away from the rain, the end of shrinking hair after a wash. It would also be the end of the painful combing of hair that was just as obstinate as the owner. It was the beginning of a new era!

By 15 identity problems became more intense (despite her long, straight hair). It wasn't really about who she was, it was more about what she represented. Her personality could have been defined as a pile of layers. On the outside she was black (and very clearly at that!). Scratch a little on the surface and the colour began to fade. Scratch a little bit more and she turned white. It was as if her personality was split between two races.

She was black because at that time she was listening mainly to hip-hop music. It was just 'cool' to be black then. She was black when racial problems were more intense, more directed towards her and what she represented. She was a "n****r" because the German/Austrian dictionary at that time defined a "n****r" as an African.

All the same, she was white because she was rejected by her Nigerian 'aunties and uncles' for her mentality. She was white because the older Nigerian generation couldn't relate to her. To them she would always be "the European girl". She was white because she hadn't yet discovered a tangible reason for being black.

At some point the reasons for being black changed. For one thing, Africans were thought to have better skin. They were known not to age as quickly as their white counterparts; they could be more creative with their hair, hence the infamous braids and weave.

In Austria the term 'black' was mostly associated with hip-hop music and basketball. Blacks were thought to be better dancers. Blacks became more popular among the white youngsters. But being black also meant facing racial discrimination and being confronted with verbal abuse from both old and young. Being black meant having to deal with immigration problems, being constantly stopped by the police for no apparent reason (as well as being battered or even killed 'accidentally' at their hands). All of which could result into anything from frustration and depression to mental illness, in extreme cases.

In this situation you would rather be white because deep down in your heart, you know that life would be easier for you. You think that you might be more accepted by your mates; you think that when you grow up you might have better chances of finding a job other than cleaning; you think that you could hold your head just a little higher when you sit on public transport without having to cope with being stared at. And you think that you would be a good deal happier with yourself. In short, your self-esteem would probably increase by half.

Today, I don't feel paranoid anymore when I get on the bus. If people stare at me, then let them stare. As long as I'm in London, it doesn't really matter. When I am back home, I console myself with the thought that it is only a temporary situation (for myself, that is). I'm not sure, though, if I have more black awareness in me.

Growing up, I wasn't told much about my origins and my knowledge was quite limited until my late-teens and early-twenties. My parents didn't have James Brown in their reservoir of albums, and I didn't get to hear the 'I'm-black-and-I'm-proud' anthem until I was well into my teens. When I did, it made no difference to the way I saw myself.

So what does that tell you about me?

I am a young Nigerian woman, born and raised in Vienna, who has been resident in London for the past six years. My Austrian-infused

English accent has faded over the years and when I speak, you could never detect that I am not England-born.

There is an interesting conclusion to this story. To the average English person I am a Londoner. To my friends and acquaintances, I am the Austrian girl who speaks exceptionally good English. And to my 'uncles and aunties', I am "the European girl".

But the tables have certainly turned. Perhaps I have more black awareness in me now than I have ever had in my young life. Perhaps I don't. To be honest with you, I couldn't care less.

Perhaps I am ignorant. After all, my state of mind has not succeeded in putting an end to racism as of yet. We can all agree that there is still prejudice and racism all over the world. But sometimes I do stop and wonder whom exactly I am supposed to protect myself from more as there is prejudice among black people too. You know the old 'fair-skinned, dark-skinned' story; the old 'skin-lightening-cream' story; the old 'I only date fair-skinned women' story. Unfortunately, I am dark-skinned.

Then there's the constant 'clash' between West Indians and Africans, or the 'clash' among Africans – the list is endless. The bottom line is that over the years, I have learnt to see myself as who I am: simply Dee. Maybe I live in a dream world because I think that by ignoring the colour of my skin I would become less confused while promoting 'world peace'.

Maybe I believe that the world would be a better place if everyone began to think like me. I know that such a belief would seem quite childish, as there is still injustice, poverty, abuse and crime present in the world. But the question is: why am I black and you white or olive-skinned? Well, why is the sky blue?

In this age of collagen lips and bottom implants, Dee appears to have those things her Caucasian sister would 'die for' and pay for – those womanly curves so typical of her origin that were once so frowned upon during her childhood and teenage years. They have suddenly become the epitome of being a woman – any woman – of the 21st century.

Did you know that 'shades' are now en vogue? Olive, tanned, fair, medium, milk chocolate, plain chocolate, even the darkest brown that bears the infamous blue undertone. The sun bed and solarium business is booming. For those who are a bit more health-conscious, fake tans in bottles are now available.

These days, white women look brown even during the coldest winter. Who would have thought some 10 or 20 years ago that being 'different' would become such an advantage? Who would have thought that society and the media would finally accept me for who I am (or attempt to, anyway)?

They even mix the right foundation for my skin tone. I can finally wear make-up without looking as if I have fallen face down into a powder pot! I am not eternally confined to wearing pink, orange or red tones on my lips anymore. If I do, it's my prerogative! I can even choose skincare that has been formulated especially for the likes of me!

But all this doesn't change who I am. Perhaps unlike many others, when I look in the mirror all I still see is Dee. What do you see?

WHAT COLOUR IS BLACK?

Tabitha Cummins

Mocha, chocolate, coffee, caramel, molasses, brown sugar, cinnamon, golden, tan, nutmeg, honey, bronze, chestnut, and ebony. These are just some of the complexions and descriptions for black skin. Black skin comes in many shades, but just what is black?

Can we really believe there is only one definition of black? Can we say that black is all down to the melanin count in your skin? If so, when does black end and white begin? Is black just defined as a colour or is there more to it than that?

If we are to believe what some parts of white society tells us, then just one drop is all it takes for someone to be black. If you have one drop of black blood then you are black, regardless of your actual skin colour or melanin count. In the eyes of some parts of white society, all it takes is one drop for you to no longer be classified as white and to become the object of scorn.

When I was growing up, there were always those white children that accepted me until parents evening after which I lost more than one friend because I not only had 'one drop' but two black parents. I always found it amusing that people could be so shallow, but it was the reality of life. White people hadn't accepted black people as equals and, therefore, contact was as limited as possible.

So what are the other criteria for being black? According to some, if you look black then you are black because that is how the world judges us – on appearance. The beautiful are judged on their looks, blondes are judged on their hair, black people are judged on their skin colour. Regardless of heritage, what you look like is what you are. So when someone of mixed origin says they are not black but mixed, there is confusion.

When I was younger there were those who would only accept me as black if I said I was mixed. That way I remained inside their comfort zone. However when the American model Veronica Webb appeared on the cover of *Pride* magazine in the 1990s, it caused division among the black community as she didn't represent what some thought a black person should looked like. In short, she was too light.

But when Tiger Woods came out later that same decade and said he was Cablasian, some of the black community again vocalised their disagreement because he clearly looked black. So why was he denying his heritage?

The division between how someone looks and what they are seems to be ever widening with the demise of segregation and the increasing popularity of mixed-race relationships. The more that people fall in love with those outside of their community, and the more the races mix, the more difficult it is to tell what race individuals are. So does this mean that there is somehow a third group appearing in the world that is neither black nor white?

If that is true that we have a third race of people emerging in the world, what happens to the Asians, Middle Easterns, Aborigines, Native Americans, South or Latin Americans? What are these people defined as? These groups have skin shades that are the same and darker than their black counterparts, but does that then mean they are black?

Some of their features would be considered white, from straight noses to straighter hair. So does being black only come down to the colour of your skin? Is it really ever that simple? If the answer is yes, then how do these groups of people categorise themselves?

You will find that most of these people accept what they are, but often it's never black. Is there something wrong with being black? Is there some negative association with being black that stops those of similar skin tones not wanting to be associated with it? Or is it that being black is more than just the colour of your skin?

The answer, I think, lies in both of those questions. It is true that as black people we face a different struggle than those of different races. After 400 years of slavery, and with racial segregation in South Africa only coming to an end in the early 1990s, it's true that negative associations with being of black African or Caribbean descent are still prevalent in today's society. However, it seems that being black is more than just what shade your skin is.

Being black has almost as much to do with what you accept about yourself as a person and your heritage. Being black is a cultural thing. It embraces more than colour and accepts more than parenting. Being black is about your state of mind as much as it is about how you are judged when someone looks at you. In a society where the mixing of the races makes the lines even more blurred, it is important to notice that black people strive forward in the many shades and colours they come in.

With the emergence of urban culture, young white people are adopting the urban black scene and wearing clothes, hair and attitudes associated with young black people. So what does that mean for today's black culture? Does it mean that we are finally being accepted as equals, or is it just a fashion trend?

As black culture develops and changes one hopes that it is not just a passing fad, but also a force to be reckoned with. As history tells us of the struggles for our acceptance in the world, we can see the emerging face of black culture more readily around us. But does this mean that it is being diluted, and that the importance of associating with your own people is dying off? Does this mean that being black is beyond culture as many other people adopt the culture? Or does this mean that these young people are black because they understand and accept the culture?

When I was growing up there were 'wiggers' at school: white kids who acted like they were 'black'. They received a tough time from both sides of the racial fence. White people thought they had sold out, stepped down or just lost their mind for associating with black people.

BEIGE: Essays

Black people thought they were wannabes and treated them as such – either as the token or the lackey. The wiggers choose to accept the culture whereas being black is something you are born with.

Has this deterred people from embracing a culture that isn't his or her own? No. Does this make that person a part of that race because they choose to accept that culture? No. If race was a choice, then at any given moment a person could change like a chameleon into something they found appropriate for the situation. Life is not that simple and no matter how we may push the boundaries and experiment with our looks, being part of a culture is not only accepting that culture, its traditions and history, but accepting the colour of your skin.

When I was young, we had black people we called Bounty or coconut. Everyone remembers them: black on the outside, white on the inside. They were the ones who accepted the white culture and became a part of it. They listened to so-called white music, had white friends and dated white people. They received as much grief as the wiggers and the price for crossing over was high. Did being a coconut make them any less black? No. Did it make people judge them any differently when they looked at them? No. To onlookers, they still saw a black person.

So being black is not only a state of mind but also the colour of your skin. But does living in Britain today mean that we can actually tell just by looking who is black? Can we, in today's culture, define at what shade black ends and white begins? I don't think, in my experience, this has ever worked. What purpose would it serve to say that black ends here and white begins there? What difference would it make to the lives of those around us?

The most passionate disputes I have heard over what colour someone is comes from those people not liberated enough to see that colour is more than just the shade of a person's skin. Genes may influence your skin colour, but it seems that God has not finished surprising the world yet.

Every day there is another child born to black parents who looks white or a dark child born to two light parents, or a mixed-looking child born to two white parents. Every day, another person accepts who they are and embraces their race regardless of what other people may say and do. Every day I look in the mirror and I see what God has blessed me with: to be a beautiful black woman even though the rest of the world may see me as white.

TESTIMONY

Katy Massey

I love this country. My country. From its scruffy urban glamour to its 'tally ho' country ways. I love the language, the humour that each ordinary person can share – especially in a disaster – and the way it never takes itself too seriously.

I have lived the length and breath of this island. I love the sunshine during the freezing Tyneside winters, when the mist sits, bad-tempered and unmovable, across the arms of the Angel of the North. Even better are the summers in Brighton, when it feels like the whole world has come out to play. Everyone smiles: big, unwieldy families from Southall and Lambeth, posh families from the Home Counties, lovelorn teenage couples and gangs of twenty-something singletons. They shop, play a game of footy on Hove Lawns, spend money on Brighton rock, smoke spliff on the beach or watch the West Pier fall gracefully into the sea.

This country, my country, taught me how to be British. Although she was a harsh teacher, and I never quite made the grade, I still long to return to her when I'm away. In extreme cases I have been known to cry with homesickness for the want of a decent cup of tea and some of my mum's mashed potato.

However, I have more than once endured the punishment of not belonging – of saying the wrong thing, laughing too loudly or not queuing properly. Then I am reminded that though I think of this as *my* country, others may disagree.

Worse still, although I love the language and its poetry, I'm aware that it is missing something fundamental. I mean, how can I write about myself when I don't have the words? My skin isn't white – if you take this to mean all the shades of flesh between putty and dark apricot. Even if you include the dark-haired, dark-eyed, olive-skin combination of the Mediterranean, that still doesn't describe me.

I am not 'swarthy' as my gran used to say, and I am not black either, if by black you mean those skin tones between milk chocolate and blue-black aubergine, stopping at molasses on the way. These are decorator's words, but they'll have to do. They are all I have.

I can't see myself from the outside, so I don't really know how others see me, especially the majority of the population who can 'wash and go'. How I envied the straight-haired women who could pull a comb through their hair without pain, and could wash and go within half an hour.

I am stuck with myself. There's no escape, but I am also bound to see myself as others see me, even if the vision I am presented with isn't me. It's just a poor approximation, a down-market impersonation. I have taken these visions inside me, turned them over, wondered about them and eventually made them a part of me – a risky business as they might be 'off'. It's unsurprising that I ended up with mood poisoning.

All because this gaze, and its demands on me, have changed the person I am. I'll try and explain. When I was very small I was cute, spoiled and clucked over more than other children: a brown baby, rare in our part of Leeds. As I got older, my colour stopped being charming and started being challenging – frightening even. Inside me, the fear became anger.

Don't get me wrong. I never had the burning anger of a rebel or revolutionary. But it has stayed alight, a small fire in my belly, bellowed by casual slights, overheard asides and dumb thoughtlessness. Awareness dawned. The awareness that my behaviour must be perfect, because you-know-what would be the reason if I was bad. Shared assumptions and opinions that had nothing to do with me but were always made *about* me. For instance, that my teeth would be strong or I could sing or be good at sport and not bookish. All of these assumptions are wrong, but why were they made in the first place?

Later at work, it would be made known to me that I had been given a 'chance'. So I must be more committed and put in more time to justify this 'chance', although I have always been more than qualified for the work I have striven to do, and do well.

Although there are no words in my own language to describe my colour, sometimes my hosts – and other guests – are less than hospitable. But I still love this country – I must be a hopeless romantic as I feel very much at home. It's a strange thing, not to have a defined 'place' or to ever really know where I belong in the 'British way of life'. Looking different is the thing of course but, despite what I have said, I don't live outside myself looking in. I am myself all of the time – at least I am what others and I have made me.

But I don't accept everything I'm told; that injustice is 'just the way it is' or 'seeing is believing'. Falling between the cracks in the language means I fall between the cracks in society. I quickly learned never to believe there is just one version of the truth. It's an exciting place to be, if a little lonely at times.

If I must describe myself, I have to borrow from Jamaican patois and say 'high yellow' is the closest phrase to describe the way I look: somewhere between gold and dark mustard. I think of it as a kind of divine brown, which gets an ashy-grey tinge in winter and a deep reddish glow if we have a good summer.

'High yellow' is a privilege on the island where my father was born and a term of abuse elsewhere. Is it also a privilege on this island, where my father died, or a curse? It's a question I have always avoided asking because though I have always loved this country, I don't know if she loves me.

SECRET FAIRIES

Ony Uhiara

Beyond the moon our land is deep,
It spreads throughout the skies.
We are the fairies, who never sleep,
But watch the world with burning eyes.

When I was younger I had this fascination with flying. Fairies and flying: that was all I thought about. I used to have a bird book, and in the centre page there was an illustration of how a bird took flight. I remember standing on the kitchen table, memorising the different stages on the page, copying the position of the bird's wings with my arms.

I really concentrated; focused. I'd try so hard to stay in the air, but in less than a second my feet were back flat on the black and red lino floor.

When I went to sleep, I used to pretend a group of fairies would take me away to play with them in the forest, and then return me to my bed in the morning before anyone awoke. I used to dream I had glittering wings and sparkling eyes. It was something I had wanted so badly. I wore flowers in my hair all the time and used to dance around instead of walk.

This craving I had, to belong to a magical world, it wasn't escape — and it wasn't anything to do with unhappiness: at least not *then*. It was just an authentic, imaginative fantasy of childhood dreams. Just to be special, filled with grace…magical.

Like I said, it was just a dream, but unhappiness soon turned it into an obsessive desire. I began to suffer in school. I started to realise and feel the pain of my skin, a totally different shade of colour to everyone else around me.

You wouldn't think that the actions and words of a child could make another child feel so out of place. But that's all it took – actions and words. Of course, the younger you are the more innocent and harmless things seem. It had started with just silly things, carefree things, but I cared. The questions developed, the comments grew. I began to feel more and more awkward. And when it came down to it, I cared a lot.

"If I hold your hand will you get me all sticky and messy with chocolate?"

"No, I won't."

"Doesn't your mum wash you?"

"Yeah, she does."

"No, that's why you're so dirty all over!"

No one wanted to sit next to me. No one wanted to stand next to me. No one wanted to touch me unless it was to spitefully pull my hair and pinch me. By the time I was in boarding school, at the age of 11, I guess I was a bit of a tearaway. Sure, I was naturally naughty, disruptive and loud in class, *but* sometimes my punishments were undeserved.

Imagine having to sit in class by yourself, while your so-called 'class mates' spat bits of wet paper at you constantly; trying to ignore it, not react, not feel. But my heartbeat would increase; my blood would fire up and the next thing I knew, I was outside the classroom with evening detention.

In the one year I spent in boarding school, I must have been called every derogatory and racist name under the sun. Of course, I had my friends, but there's only so much a group of friends who don't really understand your position can do to help. Things got worse. Some names hurt more than others. Some shoves against walls took more air out of me. I began to feel more pain.

You know that feeling when you're so frustrated and hurt you fear you might turn vicious? Well I did. I tried to resist that rush of adrenaline, but it took me over. Things would be said and I'd lash out: more fights, more punishment, more bullying. I mean *I* shouldn't have to control myself because of some idiot. *I* shouldn't have to cry in the toilets because of some fool.

I didn't want to go to sleep at night because I knew when I woke up it would be another day of feeling alone. *I* shouldn't have to suffer because of a thin layer of skin. I'd try so hard to pretend. I wanted to say, 'I don't care, it doesn't mean anything, I'm not going to cry', but sometimes I'd feel empty as if someone had stolen my words, and I couldn't speak. So I would just sit there in this enveloping, silent rage.

There was one day at school when I was coming out of class, watching the ground as I walked. One of the older boys swung his bag hard into my stomach. I fell to the floor catching the whispered "black bitch!"

I was dazed. I didn't move. A teacher came out into the corridor and saw me slumped against the wall. I ended up in the head mistress's office.

I told them everything that had happened to me since I'd arrived at the school – well nearly everything. There are certain events that an 11-year-old girl finds difficult to speak of; certain images that she has to break into pieces and bury the fragments somewhere she'll forget them. But sometimes, those fragments unearth themselves and take shape in her dreams.

Those dreams that wake you in the early hours, where everything is still and there's no blood dripping from your lip, and no boot flying into your gut. It's just you and the silence – the sound of ugly loneliness, the calm before the storm of the approaching day.

By this time I had gotten used to keeping secrets, used to not trusting those people around me. People who made such a point of letting me know how different I was. I didn't see any reason why I should make any exceptions with the teachers who I felt had often turned a blind eye anyway.

I had no naïve expectations that if I told them everything, then things would suddenly change. No, I knew I was alone. So I only told them what I allowed myself to and to be honest, part of me didn't want to give them the satisfaction of knowing I'd been knocked down so many times and in so many different ways.

I didn't want them knowing how low I'd been made to feel. Anyway, secrets and silence had become quite good friends of mine. I decided to be loyal to *them* and give my teachers the parental guidance version. So like I was saying, I told them everything!

I didn't cry though, not at all. I just left when I was done talking. It was strange though. Word must have got round the school that I was in the office of the head mistress. I hadn't mentioned any names to her, but when I came out and turned the corner the corridor walls were lined with the culprits. That's about as popular with the boys as I got. I faced my own personal bullying team!

None of the older boys looked at me. My heart fired up, and then it was still. For a second I thought about turning back into the office – yeah right! I focused on the end of the corridor and walked. My heart didn't seem to beat.

I passed the first two boys. They spat at me. I felt their spit on my skin, in my hair, on my face and clothes. The boys never said a word. They just spat out their hatred like a piece of rancid fruit. My ears filled up with that dull buzz you hear when you're underwater. In my mind's eye I imagined myself retaliating, maybe with a fist to jaw, spitting back or even a kick in the balls. But I didn't stop. I didn't lash out. I just walked down what felt like the longest corridor, ever.

At last I turned the corner, my heart and mind racing, my lungs struggling for oxygen. All of a sudden I bolted, running outside. The boys didn't follow me. No one followed me as I ran down to the sports field. No one saw me crying as I took my anger out on a tree; I proceeded to kick the trunk while beating it with my fists, the skin grazing on impact.

Still covered in the boys' spit and phlegm, I felt dirty. Wanting it all off me I started pulling at my clothes, removing them haphazardly from my body. I wrestled with my tie and jumper, using them to rub the spit from my hair, pulling off my shirt and skirt too, my uniform now lay in a sticky pile on the grass. I stood there still crying, practically naked in my long socks, knickers and thermal vest. Even though no one was around to see me, I still wanted to get out of sight. Reaching round, I clambered up into the tree and nestled in the crook of two boughs.

When I was at home, I had a thinking tree I used to sit in and pretend it was the gateway to my magical world. Now, wiping my face, I rested my head against the thick branch. I seriously thought that if the fairies were watching me they would open the gates to let me in. They would open the door and take me away because they'd see I was so sad. I sat there wishing and willing my fantasy world to reveal itself and save me... but nothing happened.

I began to fall asleep, my body was tired; my eyes felt the weight of my now exhausted tears. Sleep came and I hadn't the strength to fight it...

A glint of light pierced through my eyelids and woke me up. The sun was setting, burning orange in the sky. Sitting in the tree, the sun's light touched me, making my underdressed body warm.

Shifting, I looked down at my bare limbs: the orange from the sun glowing on my skin, turning it a golden brown. I thought – that looks nice. The more I stared at my skin, the more I believed it.

For too long I'd been told how ugly I was because I was a different colour, but now that it was just me, the tree and the sun, I saw myself differently. I realised that it didn't matter what those ignorant fools said or did because now I'd seen it for myself – and seeing is believing. I said aloud what I truly believed: "My skin looks nice."

There was a slight breeze as the sun dipped in the sky. It seemed to clear me of all the pain I had felt that day, and I felt light...... as if I could fly.

Everything was peaceful,
Everything was slow,
Because everything changes
When the wind blows.

Interviews

TONYA JOY BOLTON

"Maya Angelou has always inspired me from the age of 13 when I read '*I Know Why the Caged Bird Sings*'. She always said, I don't just survive I thrive. I think I adopted her as an auntie in my mind when I was a child. She made me feel that no matter what I went through as a human being, a woman, a black person, a spiritual person, I too can survive and thrive.

Writing began as a form of therapy for me. The first time I thought I had written something good was when I was 13. I was 20 when I started to take myself seriously, when I said yes, this is what I want to do.

I had to rethink the poems that I sent through to this anthology as they were all in CAPITALS. I don't write in capitals anymore. I only write in capitals when I want to highlight something, a particular word maybe.

I am a performance poet not a page poet, so maybe writing in capitals gave me the same feeling or effect as if I was performing the poetry live.

So far I have been published in 12 anthologies. The first time I was published was in 2001. Now, after being published in so many anthologies, I am feeling quite frustrated.

The reason being that when I perform, people come up and ask if they can buy my book. They would prefer to read my work rather than having to buy an anthology.

I don't mind anthologies, but I'm ready to publish my first collection of poetry, so '*Brown Eyes*' will probably be my last anthology.

To focus on my writing I've taken a year out of my PhD on Black Theology and Biblical Studies. I was being swallowed up by the academic world. If you are creative, not being able to write feels like suicide.

Butterfly Woman is the first poem that I ever had published. It is one of the few pieces of work where I feel the same about my position as a black spiritual woman as when I first wrote it. This is strange to me as I was 21 at the time. I'm now 27.

Butterfly Woman is about how people perceive you. I'm only 5ft. Some people perceive me as a sweet young lady or a black person or a female. In the poem I say that I'm more than just what you see. I'm also a spiritual being. Like a butterfly my identity has gone through a process of metamorphosis, a painful one, but through pain comes growth.

In the world people ask me where am I from – a lot. I say my dad is Jamaican and my mum's Cuban. I have Indian-type hair and I wear a lot of hair and face jewellery.

In Birmingham, where I live, I do feel isolated and stuck as a writer. It's all about who you know at the end of the day. A lot of writers only get recognition for their work after they have died. I hope that doesn't happen to me."

TAIYE TUKALI-WOSORNU

"*Is Black Love Dead* was the cover feature for *Drum* magazine's launch issue. The editor sent me the anthology advert and said I really think you should submit the article you wrote for us. I didn't see the advert for '*Brown Eyes*' myself.

I have always written, usually creatively and only now journalistically. The notion of my article on interracial dating reaching a wide audience is very new to my consciousness as an artist.

I'm quite a mutt. My mum is Nigerian and Scottish, born in England. My father is 110% Ghanaian, born and raised in Ghana. My twin sister and me were born in London where both of my parents were practising doctors. When they divorced my mother fled to America. I was eight. We were only meant to stay there for a short time, but she ended up marrying an American and, at 18, we were entitled to American citizenship. So now I'm a British citizen and an American citizen.

During my entire socialisation and education in the US, I was asked, 'Where are you from, you don't sound American?' When I turned 18 my mum left the States, so my sister and I went to school in America. During the holidays we would come to London. I went to Yale to study political science and now I'm at Oxford University taking a DPhil in International Relations.

The first piece I had published, for which I was paid, was called *The Drug*. I was 14-years-old. It was about children of drug users in urban America. I had grown up in a suburb and hadn't known anybody who had done drugs.

My writing teacher at Prep school asked me why I never wrote anything to do with my own life. Until I was 24, I never wrote about African people, and I almost never wrote about women. A psychologist could go to town about why that was.

When I was young, I met with success writing about white men, American mothers and working class African-Americans: all things I experienced tangentially.

So the content of *Is Black Love Dead?* was more richly personal than ever before. There is a point at which the article stops being about interracial dating and starts being about black identity, and that is where I turn up.

Being the child of African immigrants in America with brown skin entitles me to a black identity, but it also equips me to challenge what it is, has been and could be in the 'new world'.

I'm convinced that to my mum, who grew up in England with her adolescence in Nigeria, and to my father, who spent his entire formation in Africa, the concept 'black' doesn't mean anything.

To be raised by people who would never describe themselves as black in a culture that would never describe me as anything else was a project in questioning: Am I not black? Is it more important that I'm Nigerian?

Black is something that I'm dissatisfied with; the way it is used colloquially, academically and politically. But I'm also delighted about what people who are called black have done in their history. So I'm honoured to use the term, while at the same time being insistent upon complicating it."

BIOGRAPHIES

Holly Abrahams

Holly, 18, grew up in Nottingham reading the works of Mary Hoffman, Rosa Guy, Grace Nichols and Malorie Blackman. At 14 she illustrated her love of writing by compiling a personal collection of poems describing her experiences growing up. Currently studying for an Arts Foundation Diploma, she plans to study Graphic Design at university.

Bisi Akinola

Of Nigerian parentage, Bisi was born in 1972 in Derby and completed an American Studies degree at Wolverhampton University. She began to write poetry at 13-years-old. Her work has been published in *The Voice* newspaper, newsletters, several anthologies and various Internet poetry sites. She is currently teaching English to refugees and asylum seekers in London.

Deborah Akinpelu

Deborah is in her 20s and was born in Vienna, Austria. Her academic-minded parents emigrated there from Nigeria over 30 years ago. Deborah completed both her primary and secondary education in Vienna, where she was the only black student, before moving to London seven years ago to attend Middlesex University.

Daniella Blechler

Born to a Polish-English-Jewish father and a Jamaican mother, 25-year-old Daniella grew up in Hounslow, London, where she wrote her first piece at four-years-old. First published at 22, she studied comedy writing at Ealing College. Daniella is currently writing a sit com and completing an animation script. Her aim is to work in television.

Tonya Joy Bolton

Birmingham-born Tonya is a 27-year-old performance poet, writer, creative arts practitioner and teacher. She runs a successful business, delivering creative workshops to young people and women. Tonya has performed her poetry in Washington DC and throughout the UK. Published in 12 anthologies, she is completing a PhD in Black Theology and Biblical Studies.

Monique Campbell

Monique, 22, is a Black British-Jamaican who lives in south east London and writes free-verse poetry on relationships, introspection and culture. Her work appears on numerous literary Internet sites such as www.literatenubian.org and www.fiba-filmbank.org. She has completed her first novel '*Once Bad Intentions*', which she is planning to adapt into a screenplay.

Tolu Melissa Carew

Born in Lagos in December 1979, Tolu moved to London when she was 10-years-old. Her love affair with poetry began after hearing Maya Angelou's '*Phenomenal Woman*' at the age of 14. The experience led her to write the self-affirming poem Identity. "It was the first poem that spoke for me as an emerging woman."

Tania Charles

Tania lives in Northamptonshire and is of Grenadian and Bajan parentage. The 38-year-old compliance consultant has been writing poetry for six years. Her work has been published in *Poetry Now*.

Christine Collymore

Christine was born in Wellingborough, Northamptonshire, to Grenadian and Bajan parents. A mother of two, she works in mental health and has an interest in training and personal development. Now in her forties, writing has always been a major dream. "There are challenges ahead, but with spiritual guidance and support, I will continue to write."

Dorothy Cornibert du Boulay

Born 40 years ago in Dulwich, south London, Dorothy has worked extensively in the music industry, but has also been employed as a chef, publicist and corporate events producer while bringing up her daughter Nathalie. She is a part-time English teacher at Tower Hamlets College, London, and writes and performs poetry.

Tabitha Cummins

Tabitha is a 26-year-old Business Studies teacher at King Solomon High School in London. Writing since she was 15, she has largely been published in church journals and magazines. A Christian, she plays an active role in her church, working with the gospel choir as well as writing and directing plays.

Amanda Epe

Amanda was born to West African parents and raised in London. A literacy and numeracy tutor, she previously worked for British Airways as a cabin crew staff member. Amanda has an interest in travel writing and social issues, and participates in dance performance. She is planning to expand her creative writing to performance poetry.

Patricia Foster

This London-based writer, actress and educationalist has performed at literary festivals in the UK, Netherlands and America, and at venues like the Jazz Café and Bloomsbury Theatre. She has also toured in Chicago with 'Malika's Poetry Kitchen'. Patricia's work has been published in 'The Tall-lighthouse Review'. She is working on her first poetry collection.

Joy Francis

A journalist for 13 years, Joy Francis is managing director of The Creative Collective Media and co-founder of Words of Colour Productions. The former editor of *Pride* magazine is a radio and TV pundit, a published writer on mental health and a reader for the BBC's 'Get Writing' programme. She is a Fellow of the Royal Society of Arts.

Nicola Greenwood

Nicola, 29, was born in Bristol and is a Business Studies graduate. A supplier manager at a well-known bank, this previously unpublished writer says of her work: "I don't consider myself female, black or from any particular place; that is what I try to express in my poetry."

Maggie Harris

Maggie was born in Guyana and has lived in the UK since 1971. She has performed her poetry in the UK, Europe, Ireland and the Caribbean. Her first collection of poetry 'Limbolands' won the Guyana prize for Literature 2000. Her new collection of poems 'From Berbice to Broadstairs' is to be launched shortly.

Louise Hercules

Louise, 30, is a south east London-based poet and Latin American dance teacher. Born to a St Lucian mother and a Grenadian father, she has been writing poetry for the last three years. Louise's work explores the dynamics of her own identity as a young Black British woman.

Zita Holbourne

Zita has been performing as a poet for eight years. A former member of the Brothaman Poetry Collective, she is co-host and resident poet of Nu Whirled Voyces. Zita is published in numerous anthologies and has received a range of awards. She facilitates poetry workshops teaching black history and cultural awareness, and has directed poetry performances for the theatre.

Emma Louise Felicia Hopkins

Born in Grimsby, Lincolnshire in 1981, both of Emma's parents are mixed-race. Her father is Anglo-Saxon/Sierra Leonean and her mother is Lebanese/Sierra Leonean. Emma's commitment to the mixed-race perspective is central to her poetry. A Fine Art graduate, she is currently participating in her first international shows in Western and Eastern Europe.

Danielle Imbert

Danielle, 25, was born in Highbury, London to a Mauritian father and white English mother. At 16 two of her poems reached the semi finals of an international poetry competition. A graduate in Communications Culture and Media from Coventry University, Danielle is now considering her creative writing options after a five-month round the world trip.

Bianca Victoria Joseph

Bianca is the youngest contributor to this anthology. Born in 1991, her father is Dominican, her mother Italian. Bianca enjoys playing the piano, horse riding and dancing. She also likes listening to music and writing poetry. Her strongest subjects at school are English and Drama. Her anthology submission – *MIXED* – was written when she was just 11-years-old.

Jackie Lewis

Jackie left the Caribbean in the 1960s to join her parents in London. A trainer and practising psychotherapist, she is also an accomplished poet. Poetry plays a prominent part in her professional practice programme. Jackie performs her work at a range of London venues such as Congress House.

Sheree Mack

Sheree is in her early-30s, lives in Newcastle upon Tyne and is married with a six-year-old son. After teaching English for seven years, she decided to devote more time to creative writing. The creator of Identity on Tyne (a creative space for writers of colour), Sheree is completing a PhD in Black British Women Contemporary Poets.

Katy Massey

Born in Telford, Shropshire and raised in Leeds and North Yorkshire, Katy has been a journalist for over a decade, writing for titles such as the *Financial Times*, the *Evening Standard* and *Cosmopolitan*. A visiting lecturer in Journalism at Sunderland University and Newcastle University, Katy has performed her poetry across the North East.

Martha Matthews

Martha is a 36-year-old college lecturer who lives in Catford, south east London with her two sons. She has been writing for pleasure for many years, and is currently working on a collection of autobiographical short stories. Martha has been published in *Pride* magazine, and plans to make her living as a full time writer.

Lisa Maynard-Atem

A journalist, Lisa has been writing for just over a year. She has contributed to publications such as *Black Beauty and Hair Magazine* and www.preciousonline.co.uk – a website for women of colour. She also writes for the *Leeds Guide* and has been a freelance fashion stylist for three years.

Fiona McKinson

Fiona is a creative writer and freelance journalist currently studying for an MA in Journalism Studies. Her nine to five hours are spent as a communications officer. Her articles have appeared in newspapers and the Internet from *New Nation, Aspire* magazine and *London Extra* to *Tense* magazine, *Lambeth Local* news, and www.darkerthanblue.com.

Nelissa Mendy

Nelissa was born in Hackney, east London, and is the ninth of ten children. She writes and performs poetry that explores themes such as identity, spirituality, community, bereavement and self-discovery. A selection of her work has been published in '*Life, Soul and Survival*', an anthology of women writers.

Angela Morton

Born in 1976 to a Guyanese mother and an English father, Angela has two daughters – aged five and seven – and is a community nurse. Relatively new to writing, she currently writes one poem a year.

Portia Msimang

Portia, 38, lives in north London with her daughter and two cats. A graduate in Contemporary European Studies and Spanish, she writes articles for a local newspaper group. Her favourite authors include Dostoevsky and Angela Carter.

Nicki Murphy

A graduate in Drama, Theatre and Cultural Studies, Nicki is currently a student in postgraduate legal studies. Her passion for the arts developed while a member of the Carlton TV Junior Television Workshop. She gained experience in performing and directing theatre productions with small roles on children's TV. Her essay, *Labels*, is her first published work.

Hyacinth Myers

In her 30s, Hyacinth is a graduate, single parent of one, a qualified complementary therapist, artist, writer, poet and jewellery designer. Her love of writing began while at primary school, and she writes poetry in her spare time. Over the years she has had poems and articles published in journals and magazines.

Karen Plumb

Married with two school-aged sons, Karen has worked in the public sector for the past 20 years. She started writing poetry as soon as she could record her thoughts and feelings on paper. Previously unpublished, Karen is excited that her poem *Dedication* has been published in the '*Brown Eyes*' anthology.

Myrle Roach

Myrle was born 40 years ago in Montserrat. She lived there until the volcanic crisis in the mid-90s forced her and her family to relocate, first to Antigua and then the UK in 2002. She currently lives in Wellingborough, Northamptonshire. A writer of poetry, sketches and short stories, Myrle's poetry has appeared in '*Hope – Fiftieth Anniversary Anthology of Poems*', published by the University of the West Indies.

Desiree Senior

Desiree is a 27-year-old single mother of one who has been writing since primary school. A civil servant at the Foreign and Commonwealth Office, she is also a budding journalist having recently completed a Postgraduate Diploma in Magazine Journalism. She plans to combine freelance journalism with writing her first novel.

Eureka Shabazz

Eureka has five children and five grandchildren. She is also a qualified social worker, social scientist, counsellor, lecturer and writer, studying for an MA in Creative Writing and Life Writing at Goldsmith's University, London. As well as performing her poetry, with work published in several anthologies, Eureka is also a Reiki/Sekhem healer. Her new book is called 'Ancestral Healing Revelations'.

Iesha Slater

With experience in the performing arts, jazz singing and writing, 28-year-old Iesha has run drama workshops, and directed and co-ordinated plays for Black History Month. A founder of Sonsha Productions, she has qualifications in the Performing Arts, Caribbean and English Studies, and Social, Cultural and Creative Process. Iesha plans to go into creative management.

Tina Tamsho-Thomas

Manchester-born Tina is a published writer and founder of *Theatre of Colour,* which explores trans-cultural themes and celebrates the lives, experience and achievements of members of dual-heritage communities. Tina is currently working on her autobiographical play 'Dancing in Sepia Dreams', which will tour nationally and internationally in 2005.

Kim Trusty

Kim grew up in Canada and Jamaica and now lives in Birmingham. She holds a BA in Literature (Toronto's York University) and an MA in Colonial and Post-Colonial Literature (University of Warwick). Her first book of poetry, 'Darker Than Blue', was published in 2002. She is a founding member of the West Midlands poetry collective, The New October Poets.

Ony Uhiara

Ony, 25, grew up in east London and graduated as an actress from the Guildhall School of Music and Drama in 2002. Her professional stage debut in 'Fallout' by Roy Williams in 2003 at the Royal Court Theatre, led to an *Evening Standard* 'Best Newcomer' nomination. She loves writing poetry and is a self-taught musician and songwriter.

Taiye Tuakli-Wosornu

Taiye, 25, was born in London and raised in Boston. She graduated with the highest honours from Yale and Oxford, with degrees in American Studies and International Relations. Writing since the age of four, Taiye has published fiction, criticism, exposition, and poetry. Her first one-act play was produced in Oxford in 2005. She is currently finishing her debut novel.

Lynda Wireko

Writing poetry since the age of 17, Lynda finds it a "powerful tool to inspire and voice her unique journey of life" to a wider audience. Now 22 years old, Lynda has published many poems in various publications including *The Voice* and a poetry anthology 'By the light of the moon'.